Environmental Pollution and Health

NUTRITION & HEALTH

Environmental Pollution and Health

LAURIE COLLIER HILLSTROM

LUCENT BOOKS
A part of Gale, Cengage Learning

GALE
CENGAGE Learning·

Farmington Hills, Mich • San Francisco • New York • Waterville, Maine
Meriden, Conn • Mason, Ohio • Chicago

LIBRARY OF CONGRESS CATALOGING-IN-PUBLICATION DATA

Hillstrom, Laurie Collier, 1965- author.
 Environmental pollution and health / by Laurie Collier Hillstrom.
    pages cm. -- (Nutrition and health)
  Includes bibliographical references and index.
  ISBN 978-1-4205-1149-9 (hardcover)
 1. Environmental health. 2. Pollution--Health aspects. I. Title.
  RA565.H524 2015
  613'.1--dc23
                                    2015007386

Lucent Books
27500 Drake Rd.
Farmington Hills, MI 48331

ISBN-13: 978-1-4205-1149-9

Printed in the United States of America
1 2 3 4 5 6 7 19 18 17 16 15

TABLE OF CONTENTS

FOREWORD

Many people today are amazed by the amount of nutrition and health information, often contradictory, that can be found in the media. Television, newspapers, and magazines bombard readers with the latest news and recommendations. Television news programs report on recent scientific studies. The healthy living sections of newspapers and magazines offer information and advice. In addition, electronic media such as websites, blogs, and forums post daily nutrition and health news and recommendations.

This constant stream of information can be confusing. The science behind nutrition and health is constantly evolving. Current research often leads to new ideas and insights. Many times, the latest nutrition studies and health recommendations contradict previous studies or traditional health advice. When the media reports these changes without giving context or explanations, consumers become confused. In a survey by the National Health Council, for example, 68 percent of participants agreed that "when reporting medical and health news, the media often contradict themselves, so I don't know what to believe." In addition, the Food Marketing Institute reported that eight out of ten consumers thought it was likely that nutrition and health experts would have a completely different idea about what foods are healthy within five years. With so much contradictory information, people have difficulty deciding how to apply nutrition and health recommendations to their lives. Students find it difficult to find relevant, yet clear and credible information for reports.

Changing recommendations for antioxidant supplements are an example of how confusion can arise. In the 1990s antioxidants such as vitamins C and E and beta-carotene came to the public's attention. Scientists found that people who ate more antioxidant-rich foods had a lower risk of heart disease, cancer, vision loss, and other chronic conditions than those who ate lower amounts. Without waiting for more scientific study, the media and supplement companies quickly spread the word that antioxidants could help fight and prevent disease. They recommended that people take antioxidant supplements and eat fortified foods. When further scientific studies were completed, however, most did not support the initial recommendations. While naturally occurring antioxidants in fruits and vegetables may help prevent a variety of chronic diseases, little scientific evidence proved antioxidant supplements had the same effect. In fact, a study published in the November 2008 *Journal of the American Medical Association* found that supplemental vitamins A and C gave no more heart protection than a placebo. The study's results contradicted the widely publicized recommendation, leading to consumer confusion. This example highlights the importance of context for evaluating nutrition and health news. Understanding a topic's scientific background, interpreting a study's findings, and evaluating news sources are critical skills that help reduce confusion.

Lucent's Nutrition and Health series is designed to help young people sift through the mountain of confusing facts, opinions, and recommendations. Each book contains the most recent up-to-date information, synthesized and written so that students can understand and think critically about nutrition and health issues. Each volume of the series provides a balanced overview of today's hot-button nutrition and health issues while presenting the latest scientific findings and a discussion of issues surrounding the topic. The series provides young people with tools for evaluating conflicting and ever-changing ideas about nutrition and health. Clear narrative peppered with personal anecdotes, fully documented primary and secondary source quotes, informative sidebars, fact boxes, and statistics are all used to help readers understand these topics and how they affect their bodies and their lives. Each volume includes information about changes in trends over time, political controversies, and international perspectives. Full-color photographs and charts enhance all volumes in the series. The Nutrition and Health series is a valuable resource for young people to understand current topics and make informed choices for themselves.

The Connection Between Pollution and Health

Fresh air, pure water, and clean land seem like basic ingredients for a healthy life. In an ideal world, people would live in perfect harmony with their natural surroundings. In the real world, however, people often make choices in their use of natural resources that have a negative impact on the health of the planet and its inhabitants. Many everyday human activities—such as heating homes, driving cars, taking showers, and disposing of waste—contribute to pollution, or the introduction of potentially damaging contaminants into the environment. Pollution can take the form of manmade chemical substances, such as pesticides; naturally occurring biological agents, like the bacterium *E. coli*; or energy, including light, heat, noise, and radiation. Harmful pollutants can contaminate the air people breathe, the water they drink, the food they eat, and the soil they walk on.

According to the World Health Organization (WHO), air pollution contributes to 7 million early deaths worldwide each year. Inhaling toxic chemicals and other contaminants increases the risk of stroke, heart disease, lung disease, and various forms of cancer. Air pollution is also linked to asthma, a chronic lung disorder that affects one out of every eleven American children—more than twice as many as in 1980. "The risks from air pollution are now far greater than previously thought or understood," said Maria Neira, WHO's public health director. "Few risks have a greater impact on global health today than air pollution; the evidence signals the need for concerted action to clean up the air we all breathe."[1]

Water pollution kills an estimated twenty-five thousand people around the world every day. Most of them die from preventable diarrheal diseases, and about 90 percent are children under the age of five. Although the problem is most severe in developing countries—due to poverty, poor sanitation and waste management practices, and weak environmental laws—it also affects the United States and many other wealthy nations. The outdated sewer system in the city of London, England, for instance, releases raw sewage into the River Thames whenever it rains heavily. In the United States, the Environmental Protection Agency (EPA) estimates that 850 billion gallons (3.2 trillion L) of raw sewage enters water bodies each year, causing millions of people to develop skin rashes, intestinal illnesses, and other health problems.

Another serious health concern involves the toxic chemicals that are contained in so many everyday products—from toys and clothing to toothpaste and dish soap. U.S. consumption of chemicals has increased by more than 8,200 percent since 1980, yet only 1 percent of the chemicals on the market have been fully tested for their effects on human health. "The production and use of synthetic chemicals has vastly outpaced our ability to monitor their effects on our health and the environment," McKay Jenkins wrote in *What's Gotten into Us?* "We learned to love what chemicals could make; we just never bothered to wonder if there could be a downside."[2]

Studies have shown that people's exposure to chemicals begins before they are even born. When the American Red Cross tested blood from the umbilical cords of ten newborn babies in 2004, they found 287 different toxins, including 180 that are known to cause cancer, 217 that are harmful to the brain and nervous system, and 208 that cause birth defects in animal studies. Many scientists blame exposure to harmful chemicals for rising rates of premature birth, learning disabilities, poor motor skills, ADHD, autism, obesity, and cancer. "Ironically, by becoming so familiar a presence

A commuter in Beijing, China, wears a mask to protect herself from high levels of smog in October 2014.

among children, these disorders now appear almost normal or inevitable," biologist Sandra Steingraber wrote in *Raising Elijah*. "While environmental factors are not the only cause of [these health problems], they are unquestionably contributing to them, and they are preventable."[3]

As the world's population continues to grow and more people squeeze into crowded urban areas, exposure to environmental pollution is expected to increase. In addition, new health risks associated with pollution are likely to be uncovered. It will require a determined global effort to reverse the effects of pollution and preserve the health of both people and the environment. "As governments around the globe are establishing air and water emission limits, individuals too need to come forward and join the clean earth campaign," according to the United Nations Environment Programme. "As a society we produce, use, and dispose of far more chemicals than ever. It's time we realized that this is not the legacy we are supposed to leave behind for our children to inherit."[4]

CHAPTER 1

Air Pollution and Health

Since all living things need air in order to survive, the cleanliness and quality of the air in the earth's atmosphere is very important. Air pollution refers to the release of substances into the air that would not normally be present and that are potentially harmful to the health of human beings or the environment. Common air pollutants include smoke, soot, dust, nitrogen oxides, sulfur oxides, carbon monoxide, hydrocarbons, and metals. Hazardous or toxic air pollutants are substances that may cause cancer or other serious health effects, such as birth defects, or wreak severe ecological damage.

Although it may seem like a fairly recent phenomenon, air pollution has existed since early human history. When people first began using fire for heat and cooking, for instance, they produced smoke that polluted the air. Industrialization led to tremendous improvements in the standard of living for many people, with the introduction of new methods of power generation, manufacturing, and transportation. But the many factories, mills, mines, and railways that sprung up during the 1800s also led to vast increases in the amount of manmade pollutants that entered the environment. In the twentieth century, air pollution from automobiles, industrial processes, and the burning of coal in power plants and homes multiplied to such an extent that it posed a threat to human health.

Episodes of "smog" (a combination of smoke and fog) in large cities like New York and London resulted in many deaths during the nineteenth century, and air pollution continued to be a significant problem through the middle of the twentieth century. In 1952, for instance, an event known as the Great Smog claimed the lives of four thousand people in London. Most of the city's 8 million residents used coal fires to heat their homes at that time. During certain weather conditions, residents claimed the resulting smog was as thick as pea soup. The Great Smog hung over London for five days, reducing visibility to less than 2 feet (.6m) and bringing all activity in the city to a standstill. According to the British National Society for Clean Air and Environmental Protection, this event "marks the dividing line between the general acceptance of air pollution as a natural consequence of industrial development, and the understanding that progress without pollution control is no progress at all."[5] Londoners responded to the frightening event by demanding that their government take action to improve air quality in the city.

The worst air pollution disaster in U.S. history occurred in October 1948 in Donora, Pennsylvania, a small industrial town in the Monongahela River valley about 25 miles (40km) outside of Pittsburgh. Residents had grown accustomed to a yellowish haze hanging in the morning air over the town's steel mill, zinc plant, and railroad yard. "The smog created a burning sensation in your throat and eyes and nose," recalled Charles Stacey, who was a high school student at that time, "but we still thought that was just normal for Donora."[6] On this occasion, however, weather conditions trapped a toxic mix of carbon monoxide, sulfur dioxide, fluorine, and metal dust in the valley for five straight days. Twenty people died of respiratory illnesses and more than seven thousand became seriously ill as a result of the severe air pollution.

Like the Great Smog, the Donora tragedy helped raise public awareness of the connection between air pollution

and health. Once Americans realized that the smog increasingly present in their cities and towns could be deadly, they demanded that legislators take steps to address the problem. This concern led to passage of the Air Pollution Control Act of 1955, which provided federal funding for research into the major sources of air pollution. Congress later incorporated this data into the Clean Air Act of 1970 (CAA), which established the National Ambient Air Quality Standards and placed limits on emissions of various types of pollutants from industrial facilities and automobiles. The CAA underwent major revisions in 1977 and 1990 to address newly recognized air pollution problems such as acid rain and holes in the atmospheric ozone layer.

Despite such measures, smog can still be a problem in large cities, especially those that have a warm, dry climate, experience heavy motor vehicle traffic, and are located in areas surrounded by mountains. Some of the cities that

Pedestrians walk through Piccadilly Circus in London, England, engulfed by heavy smog in December 1952. The Great Smog of 1952 killed thousands of people in England and severely impaired transportation because of the lack of visibility.

have struggled with poor air quality and persistent smog in the twenty-first century include New Delhi, India; Beijing, China; Mexico City, Mexico; Santiago, Chile; and Cairo, Egypt. In 2014, air pollution in New Delhi reached levels sixty times higher than what was considered safe, yet the number of cars on the densely populated city's streets increased by 1,400 a day, adding exhaust fumes to smoke from burning garbage and emissions from factories and coal-fired power plants. As a result of this toxic mix, two out of every five residents of New Delhi suffers from respiratory illnesses.

Sources of Air Pollution

A key to improving air quality and preventing health problems is understanding the sources of air pollution. Some types of air pollutants originate from natural sources, such as wind-blown dust and pollen, smoke from wildfires, and ash from volcanoes. Although natural sources sometimes generate significant amounts of air pollution, the effects are usually temporary and do not create long-term problems. Most of the hazardous air pollutants that cause health problems come from regular human activity. The sources of toxic pollutants can be classified as point sources or nonpoint sources.

Point source pollution originates with a single source that can be easily identified. Examples of point source pollution include air pollution from the smokestack of a coal-fired power plant, water pollution from the discharge pipe of a sewage treatment plant, noise pollution from a jet engine, and light pollution from an illuminated billboard. Point sources are also known as stationary sources because they tend to remain in one place, which generally makes it easier to monitor, measure, and control their emissions than is the case with other sources of pollution. On the other hand, once toxic air pollutants are released from a factory, refinery, power plant, or other point source, they can travel long distances and contribute to health problems over large geographical areas.

Nonpoint source pollution, by contrast, cannot be traced to one specific source. Instead, it comes from multiple smaller sources that are spread over a wide area. Examples of nonpoint source pollution include air pollution from car tailpipes or water pollution from urban runoff (rainwater washing contaminants off of roads, parking lots, and yards and depositing them in lakes and rivers). Nonpoint source pollution stems from the activities of many different people, which makes it much more difficult to measure and regulate than point source pollution. Some nonpoint sources of air pollution are known as mobile sources because they move around—such as cars, trucks, buses, trains, and airplanes. Other nonpoint sources of air pollution are known as area sources, because they encompass activities occurring throughout a certain area—such as the smoke emitted from all the fireplaces and barbeques in a neighborhood, or the methane gas produced by all the livestock in an agricultural region.

According to the U.S. Environmental Protection Agency (EPA), the transportation sector accounts for more than half of all the air pollution in the United States. The other main

Exhaust from vehicle tailpipes is an example of nonpoint source pollution, which comes from multiple, smaller sources spread over a wide area.

producers of air pollution include power generation facilities that burn fossil fuels, industrial factories—especially those that make metals, plastics, or chemicals—and garbage incinerators.

Types of Air Pollutants

Many different substances can be considered air pollutants if they reach a level of concentration that is high enough to cause harm. The EPA regulates 187 different substances that it classifies as hazardous air pollutants because of their potential to harm human health or the environment. Some of the substances that are controlled under the Clean Air Act Amendments of 1990 include mercury, benzene, dioxin, and asbestos. Although all of these substances can be dangerous, the EPA has established national ambient air standards for six common "criteria pollutants" that cause concern:

Sulfur dioxide (SO$_2$): Sulfur is an impurity that is often present in hydrocarbon "fossil" fuels like coal and petroleum. When these fuels are burned, the sulfur combines with oxygen in the air to produce sulfur dioxide. Coal-fired power plants are the primary source of SO$_2$ pollution, which contributes to smog and acid rain.

Carbon monoxide (CO): This colorless, odorless, tasteless gas is produced when hydrocarbon fuels like gasoline lack enough oxygen to burn completely. It is present in motor vehicle exhaust and can reach dangerous levels inside homes with a poorly maintained gas appliance, such as a furnace, stove, or water heater. CO is toxic to humans because it combines with hemoglobin in the bloodstream, preventing it from carrying needed oxygen to organs and tissues.

Nitrogen oxides (NO$_x$): Nitrogen oxide (NO) and nitrogen dioxide (NO$_2$) are part of a family of highly reactive gases called nitrogen oxides (NO$_x$). These gases are formed during combustion, or burning of fuel. The main sources of NO$_x$ air pollutants are motor vehicle exhaust and electrical power plants. NO$_2$ reacts in the air to form toxic organic nitrates and highly corrosive nitric acid. It also plays a major role in the atmospheric reactions that produce ground-level ozone, smog, and acid rain.

Particulate matter (PM): These tiny particles, which may be solid or liquid in form, are considered pollutants when they become suspended in air. Airborne particulates can come from natural sources—such as leaf litter, pollen, ocean salt, sand, dust, or volcanic ash—or from human activities, like motor vehicle traffic, construction, or farming. The health risk associated with particulates depends on their size. Large particles, like grains of sand, can be irritating, but they are not readily inhaled and settle out of the air quickly. Of much greater concern are coarse particles of less than 10 microns in diameter (designated as PM10) and fine particles of less than 2.5 microns in diameter (PM2.5), which can penetrate deep into the lungs and pose significant health risks. Ultrafine particles of less than 0.1 micron in diameter are even more dangerous because they can pass through lung tissue and enter the bloodstream.

Ozone (O_3): Unlike conventional oxygen (O_2), which is made up of two oxygen atoms joined together, ozone is composed of three oxygen atoms. Ozone is not a primary pollutant that is emitted directly into the atmosphere. Instead, it is a secondary pollutant that is produced when sunlight reacts with other pollutants, including nitrogen dioxide and unburned hydrocarbons. In the upper atmosphere, ozone forms a protective layer that screens out harmful ultraviolet radiation from the sun. At ground level, however, ozone is a toxic pollutant that contributes to the formation of smog and to various health problems.

Lead and heavy metals: These toxic compounds can be spread into the air as particulate matter or dispersed through gases in aerosol form. They are present in motor vehicle exhaust fumes and in ash from incinerator smokestacks.

NUTRITION FACT

3

The number of times more likely that toxic chemicals in the home are to cause cancer than outdoor air pollution

Smoke billows out of a steel mill in France. Industrial processes such as paper production, petroleum refining, and iron and steel manufacturing account for a significant amount of the particulate matter released into the atmosphere.

Many of the air pollutants of concern are strongly related to burning hydrocarbons or fossil fuels. The main sources of these pollutants are motor vehicles, power generation facilities, garbage incinerators, and furnaces in homes and buildings. Motor vehicle emissions have the greatest impact on ambient air quality in cities because the exhaust fumes are released close to the ground, where people are more likely to inhale them, and are slow to disperse from narrow streets between tall buildings.

In addition to the air pollution created by the combustion of fuels, some pollutants are released into the environment as part of consumable products, such as volatile organic compounds (VOCs) in solvents, paints, waxes, varnishes, and glues. VOCs contribute to the formation of ozone and smog, and some of them can cause cancer or other long-term health problems when inhaled. Other pollutants are released into the atmosphere as byproducts of industrial processes or through accidental leakage. Vast amounts of particulate matter, for instance, come from petroleum refineries, iron and steel mills, pulp and paper mills, chemical plants, and cement and asphalt plants.

Indoor Air Pollution

When most people think about air pollution, they envision car exhaust fumes, factory smokestacks, and smog—all of which affect air quality outdoors. Yet a number of toxic substances often pollute the air inside of homes and buildings. In fact, harmful pollutants can reach high concentrations indoors when homes and buildings are tightly sealed or poorly ventilated. Indoor air pollution is a major problem in developing countries, where people are more likely to burn wood or coal to cook food and heat their homes. But it can also be a problem in highly developed countries, where people commonly use paint, glue, cleansers, insulation, and other household chemicals that release pollutants into the air.

One of the biggest causes of indoor air pollution is secondhand smoke. Cigarette smoking releases hundreds of toxic chemicals, including seventy that are known to cause cancer. It poses a serious health risk not only to smokers, but also to nonsmokers who live or work with people who smoke. Exposure to secondhand smoke causes 34,000 premature deaths from heart disease and 7,300 from lung cancer in the United States each year. It is especially dangerous for children, contributing to asthma, respiratory illnesses, ear infections, and sudden infant death syndrome (SIDS). Many businesses and communities have established smoke-free workplaces and public spaces in an effort to address this problem.

Another serious threat to indoor air quality comes from carbon monoxide, which can pollute homes through

Cigarette smoke is one of the biggest causes of indoor air pollution.

car exhaust fumes or broken gas appliances. Exposure to carbon monoxide can cause symptoms including headache, fatigue, and loss of consciousness, and it can be deadly in high concentrations. Since the gas is impossible to see or smell, home safety experts recommend installing carbon monoxide detectors. Radon is another invisible, odorless gas that poses a safety risk to homes, offices, and schools. This radioactive gas is produced naturally through the decay of uranium in soil and rock. It usually enters buildings by seeping through concrete foundations and basements, where it becomes trapped and reaches high levels of concentration. Exposure to radon causes twenty-one thousand deaths from lung cancer in the United States each year, although there are inexpensive testing kits and reduction systems available.

Asbestos is another substance that has been linked to lung cancer. This fibrous molecule was once widely used in construction for its insulation and fireproofing properties. Although scientists learned in the 1970s that it was a carcinogen (cancer-causing agent), by that time asbestos was present in millions of homes and buildings. Since asbestos does not pose a hazard unless its fibers are inhaled, experts continue to debate whether it is best to remove it or leave it undisturbed. Still other toxic chemicals, like formaldehyde, are widely used in dyes and glues for carpeting and upholstery. As they are gradually released into the air, these chemicals can cause irritation of the eyes, nose, throat, and skin.

"Leukemia High School"

Port Neches, with a population of thirteen thousand residents, is an industrial town lined with oil refineries, chemical plants, and rubber factories on the Gulf Coast of Texas. Up until the Clean Air Act Amendments of 1990 regulated emissions of butadiene, the Texaco West chemical plant in Port Neches released 1.1 million pounds (500,000kg) of the carcinogenic substance into the air annually. A report by the U.S. Environmental Protection Agency once claimed that this industrial facility posed a greater potential cancer risk to people living nearby than any other in the United States. It estimated the lifetime risk of cancer for those living closest to the plant to be 1 in 10, which is 100,000 times higher than normal.

Port Neches–Groves High School is located adjacent to the Texaco West facility. Between 1963 and 1993, there were twenty-six confirmed cases of leukemia, lymphoma, and related cancers among current or former students at the school. The unusually high incidence of cancer among the student population caused critics to label the school "Leukemia High." Teri N. Segura, a 1994 graduate of the school, developed a cancerous brain tumor that she blamed on exposure to butadiene as a student.

Despite the health risks from persistent air pollution, however, many residents of Port Neches are hesitant to complain. The town's economy depends almost entirely on the industrial facilities, so some people worry that strict emission control would cause plants to close and people to lose their jobs.

Up to 30 percent of newly constructed buildings develop something known as sick building syndrome. In these buildings, inadequate ventilation and poor indoor air quality combine to cause health problems for inhabitants, including headaches, nausea, dizziness, fatigue, and difficulty concentrating. Although the causes vary, experts usually blame toxic chemicals in building materials—such as carpeting, flooring, upholstery, wiring, and insulation—along with biological hazards like mold. Sick building syndrome can be difficult and expensive to resolve, so it is important for builders to choose nontoxic materials and install adequate air filtration systems.

Health Effects of Air Pollution

Whether indoors or outdoors, air pollution has the potential to harm human health. The health risk associated with air pollution depends on the type of pollutant, the amount of exposure, and the individual person. The EPA publishes data about the known health effects of each type of air pollutant covered under the Clean Air Act in its *Health Effects Notebook for Hazardous Air Pollutants*, available online at http://www.epa.gov/ttn/atw/hlthef/hapindex.html. The agency also provides information about the levels of pollution exposure faced by residents of different areas in its *National Air Toxics Assessment*, available online at http://www.epa.gov/ttn/atw/natamain/. Certain characteristics make some people more vulnerable to health effects from exposure to air pollution than others. In general, the following categories of people are most likely to suffer harmful health effects:

- young people (infants, children, and teenagers);
- elderly people (those over sixty-five years of age);
- people with lung diseases (such as asthma, bronchitis, or emphysema) or heart disease;
- people with low incomes;
- people who work outdoors or are very active outdoors in polluted areas.

Some health effects from exposure to air pollution are temporary, reversible, and not life-threatening. While stand-

ing behind a bus and inhaling exhaust fumes, for instance, a person might experience such symptoms as burning eyes, a scratchy throat, wheezing, or coughing. In most cases, the affected person will feel better as soon as they leave the polluted area. The health effects from long-term exposure to air pollution, however, are often permanent, irreversible, and life-threatening. These effects include:

- increased risk and severity of asthma attacks and respiratory infections;
- increased susceptibility to inflammation of the lung tissue and development of chronic obstructive pulmonary disease (COPD);
- increased risk of cardiovascular diseases, including heart attacks, strokes, and congestive heart failure;
- increased risk of premature death from respiratory and cardiovascular causes;
- increased mortality in infants and young children;
- increased risk of reproductive harm and developmental problems.

Boys play soccer at a park covered by smog in New Delhi, India, in 2012. Young people have a higher risk of developing illnesses related to air pollution.

Although many of the risks associated with air pollution come from breathing contaminated air, people's health can be affected through other means as well. Toxic air pollutants can settle on plants or be deposited in soil or water. In this way, these hazardous substances can contaminate animals that feed on contaminated plants, fruits and vegetables that are grown in contaminated soil, or fish that swim in contaminated water. Persistent toxic air pollutants can accumulate in body tissues and reach higher and higher concentrations as they are consumed by people and animals at the top of the food chain.

One way in which air pollutants damage the environment is through acid rain. Acid rain occurs when nitrogen oxides and sulfur dioxide emitted from power plants and factories react with other compounds in the atmosphere to create nitric acid and sulfuric acid. These chemicals are then washed out of the air by rainfall, which becomes more acidic than normal. Acid rain emerged as a major problem in North America in the 1950s. In some U.S. and Canadian cities, it destroyed trees and crops, stripped paint off cars, and ruined historic buildings, especially those made of marble. It also acidified lakes and streams, killing many species of aquatic life, such as fish and frogs. Efforts to control sulfur emissions have helped to reduce the problems associated with acid rain in the twenty-first century.

Air Pollution Control Laws and Strategies

The Clean Air Act is the primary legislation governing air pollution in the United States. Under the original 1970 framework and later amendments, the EPA maintains national ambient air quality standards for a whole list of pollutants and requires states to meet them by using the latest science and technology. Implementation of the CAA led to a 72 percent reduction in national emissions of the common pollutants of concern between 1970 and 2012—despite the fact that during the same period, the U.S. population grew by 53 percent and national energy consumption increased by 47 percent. Reducing air pollution not only cleaned up

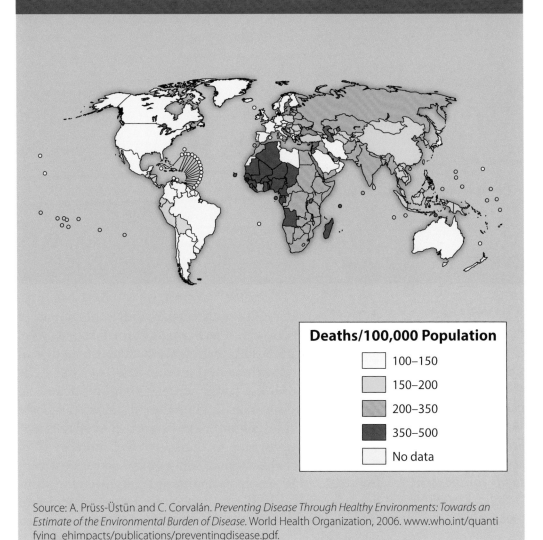

DEATHS ATTRIBUTED TO ENVIRONMENTAL POLLUTION AROUND THE WORLD

Deaths/100,000 Population

- 100–150
- 150–200
- 200–350
- 350–500
- No data

Source: A. Prüss-Üstün and C. Corvalán. *Preventing Disease Through Healthy Environments: Towards an Estimate of the Environmental Burden of Disease.* World Health Organization, 2006. www.who.int/quanti fying_ehimpacts/publications/preventingdisease.pdf.

the environment but also improved citizens' health. An EPA report to Congress found that pollution reductions under the 1990 CAA amendments prevented 205,000 early deaths and millions of other health effects within the first year they took effect.

A scrubber can be seen near the bottom of a smokestack at a coal-fired power plant in Winfield, West Virginia. Scrubbers help power plants reduce sulfur emissions, in compliance with the Clean Air Act.

The Clean Air Act regulates many different sources of air pollution. Coal-fired power plants, for instance, were required to reduce sulfur emissions that contribute to acid rain, smog, and various health problems. They did so by using coal with lower sulfur content, adopting clean coal technologies to separate out the sulfur, installing scrubbers on smokestacks to capture sulfur before it entered the environment, and switching to alternative fuel sources. All of these methods helped reduce sulfur emissions by 35 percent from 1973 to 1997, which significantly improved the problem of acid rain in the United States. However, acid rain remains a serious problem in other parts of the world, such as China.

Other industries have made strides toward reducing air pollution to meet EPA standards as well. New factories are built with modern pollution-control technologies, while older facilities are modified to reduce emissions. As a result, American stationary sources release 1.5 million tons (1.4 million t) less toxic pollution per year than they did in 1990. Mobile sources of air pollution, including automobiles,

Air Pollution and the Ozone Layer

Although it is considered a pollutant at ground level, ozone (O_3) in the earth's atmosphere plays an important role in screening out harmful ultraviolet radiation from the sun. In the late 1970s, scientists discovered giant holes in the protective ozone layer above Antarctica and the Arctic. They traced the source of the holes to air pollution from ozone-depleting chemicals called chlorofluorocarbons (CFCs), which were commonly used as coolants in refrigerators and air conditioners and as propellants in aerosol sprays.

The depletion of ozone in the atmosphere allows more sunlight to reach the surface of the earth, where it damages trees and crops and can lead to cataracts and skin cancer. In fact, for every 1 percent decrease in atmospheric ozone, scientists found a 1 to 2 percent increase in malignant melanoma, a deadly form of skin cancer, and a much larger increase in nonmalignant skin cancers, such as basal cell carcinoma and squamous cell carcinoma.

In response to this global health threat, leaders of 168 nations signed an agreement called the Montreal Protocol of 1987, which established strict limits on the production and use of CFCs and other ozone-depleting substances. Thanks to this and later treaties, the level of ozone in the atmosphere has been increasing since 1998 and is expected to reach pre-1980 levels within fifty years.

A large ozone hole over Antarctica is shown in dark blue in this NASA satellite image from 2005.

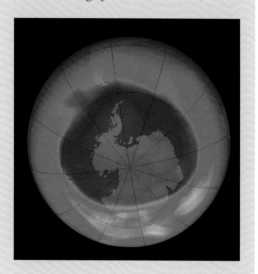

have also become much cleaner under the CAA. Improvements in engine technology—such as catalytic converters that capture carbon monoxide and nitrogen dioxide—and cleaner-burning fuels have helped reduce tailpipe emissions of common pollutants from new cars and trucks by 99 percent from 1970 levels.

Although the United States has made great strides since the 1970s toward reducing air pollution, many areas still exceed national air quality standards for at least one of the six common pollutants. Probably the most problematic air pollutants in the twenty-first century are ozone and particulate matter, both of which are emitted from diverse sources and travel long distances, making them difficult to regulate. Exposure to some forms of air pollution is inevitable, but there are ways to limit the health risks. For instance, both ozone and particle pollution levels tend to be highest in the afternoon heat, so experts recommend staying indoors at this time of day and scheduling outdoor activities for the early morning or evening hours.

CHAPTER 2

Water Pollution and Health

A lthough water covers nearly three-quarters of the surface of the earth, only 1 percent of that total is freshwater that is available for people to use. The rest is salt water contained in the world's oceans or frozen water trapped in polar ice caps and mountain glaciers. The freshwater held in lakes, ponds, rivers, streams, reservoirs, and underground aquifers must support 7 billion people. The World Health Organization (WHO) estimates that each person needs a minimum of 5 gallons (20L) of water per day to meet their basic needs for drinking, washing, and sanitation (disposing of waste). An average American uses close to 100 gallons (380L) of water per day for these purposes. Between water pollution and water shortages, however, an estimated 1 billion people worldwide do not have reliable access to a safe, fresh water supply.

In addition to drinking, people also use water for a wide range of other purposes, such as irrigation, manufacturing, transportation, power generation, and recreation. But many human activities generate pollution that gets into water supplies and reduces the quality of this valuable resource. All over the world, up to 2 million tons (1.8 million t) of waste and chemicals are dumped into lakes and rivers every day. Water pollution is a difficult and expensive problem

A polluted waterway runs by a market in Cochin, Kerala, India. Water pollution poses a serious threat to human health, especially in developing countries.

to reverse, and it poses a direct threat to human health. In fact, WHO attributes eight out of every ten illnesses in the world to unsafe water or poor sanitation.

Although the majority of waterborne illnesses affect people in developing countries, water pollution is a public health issue even in developed countries like the United States. The U.S. Environmental Protection Agency (EPA) indicates that 64 percent of lakes and ponds and 44 percent of rivers and streams across the country have levels of pollution that make them unfit for swimming and fishing. In addition, 10 percent of Americans have been exposed to unsafe drinking water, and 19.5 million people get sick every year from drinking water that contains harmful microorganisms.

Raising Public Awareness of Water Pollution

Water pollution has created health risks ever since large populations of people began living in cities. Early urban centers lacked facilities to handle the massive volumes of garbage and excrement produced by their residents, so much of this material ended up being dumped in nearby waterways. The polluted water became breeding grounds for bacteria and viruses, so epidemics of waterborne diseases such as cholera and typhoid fever struck the people who relied upon it for drinking and bathing.

A cholera outbreak that hit New York City in 1832, before people had a good understanding of sanitation and the role of germs in disease, killed 3,500 residents in the overcrowded city of 250,000. Anyone with the means and opportunity to flee the city did so, leaving the streets virtually empty. "There is no business doing here except that done by Cholera: Doctors, Undertakers, Coffinmakers, &c," wrote a man who lived near the center of the outbreak. "Our bustling city now wears a most gloomy & desolate aspect—one may take a walk up & down Broadway & scarce meet a soul."[7] City officials responded to this tragic event by constructing an aqueduct system to carry clean water from upstate and banning pigs and other livestock from neighborhoods. Nevertheless, similar outbreaks continued until public health officials began treating municipal drinking water with chlorine to kill germs in the early 1900s.

As cities became more industrialized, mines, mills, and factories dumped chemicals and waste products into waterways, including hazardous substances like sulfuric acid, soda ash, muriatic acid, lime, dyes, wood pulp, and animal byproducts. The combination of toxic chemicals, sewage, and garbage turned many lakes, rivers, and harbors into reeking messes. Still, few Americans expressed concern about water pollution because they viewed it as a necessary consequence of the industrial growth that created jobs and economic prosperity.

This outlook changed in 1969, when *Time* magazine ran a startling photograph that showed flames leaping from the surface of the Cuyahoga River in Cleveland, Ohio. The accompanying story described the river as "chocolate-brown, oily, bubbling with subsurface gases" and said that it "oozes rather than flows."[8] Many Americans were alarmed by the idea that water could be so heavily polluted that it caught on fire, and they demanded that the federal government take action. Increasing public environmental awareness and concern about water pollution led to passage of the Clean Water

Firemen battle a fire as it spreads across the Cuyahoga River near Cleveland, Ohio, in 1952. Photos of the fire-prone, heavily polluted river published in Time *magazine spurred implementation of the Clean Water Act.*

Act in 1972. This legislation provides the basis for regulating pollutant discharges and ensuring water quality in the United States.

Sources of Water Pollution

Regulating water pollution is difficult because it comes from so many different sources. Like air pollution, the sources of water pollution can be divided into two main categories: point sources and nonpoint sources. Point source pollution comes from a single, identifiable source, such as an oil refinery, paper mill, or chemical factory. Some factories discharge contaminated water, known as effluents, directly into lakes or rivers, while others have their own water treatment facilities on site to remove debris or harmful chemicals. Still other industrial operations release their effluents into municipal sewer systems or send them to sewage treatment plants for processing.

Sewage treatment plants handle both industrial wastewater and human waste from homes and businesses. They use various processes to remove physical, chemical, and biological contaminants before releasing environmentally safe, treated water into a river, lake, or ocean. Unfortunately, many cities' sewage treatment systems are old and in disrepair, while others are overstressed by the demands of rapidly growing populations. As a result, 37 percent of the twenty-five thousand sewage treatment plants in the United States—and 90 percent of those in developing nations—have released raw, untreated sewage into natural bodies of water.

In contrast to point source pollution discharged by sewage treatment plants or factories, nonpoint source water pollution consists of small amounts of pollutants that are released by many different sources, such as septic tanks, cars, trucks, boats, farms, ranches, and forest areas. Most nonpoint source water pollution occurs as runoff. During times of rain or melting snow, water flows across city streets and parking lots, suburban lawns and driveways, and rural fields and forests. The stormwater picks up dirt, leaves, oil, gasoline, fertilizers, pesticides, salt, animal waste, and other contaminants as it runs off these surfaces. This untreated runoff, which can

contain many harmful substances, eventually makes its way into storm drains, lakes, or rivers.

The EPA estimates that agriculture is responsible for 70 percent of water pollution in the United States. Depending on their size and type, farming operations can be either point or nonpoint sources of water pollution. Large, commercial farms that raise livestock such as cows, pigs, turkeys, and chickens generate huge amounts of animal wastes. The largest of these operations, which are defined and regulated under the Clean Water Act as concentrated animal feeding operations (CAFOs), must develop plans for managing their wastewater. Manure, urine, and other organic waste materials are often held in open lagoons until they can be treated or disposed of—sometimes by spraying the mixture on fields as a fertilizer. Lagoon leakage, overflow, or runoff can allow raw sewage to contaminate nearby bodies of water as a point source of pollution.

Tracts of land that are used to grow crops can be considered nonpoint sources of water pollution. Plowing the land

Poisoned by Well Water

Hydraulic fracturing, or "fracking," is a process used in the energy industry to extract natural gas from underground shale deposits. Critics of fracking claim that it has the potential to pollute groundwater with toxic chemicals. One of these critics is John Barnes of Masontown, Pennsylvania. He tells the harrowing story of his thirty-two-year-old niece, who became severely ill and fell into a coma in 2009 after a natural gas well was drilled 200 feet (61m) away from her water well. "The doctors hadn't a clue as to what caused her to enter this comatose state," he recalls. "Her liver failed and her lungs were filled with fluid and had to be drained. She had pneumonia along with impaired kidney and heart functions. Her heart valves had been encrusted by an unknown foreign body."

Although Barnes's niece emerged from the coma after several weeks, her health remained precarious. Doctors eventually discovered that her blood contained barium—one of the toxic chemicals used in fracking—at a level eleven times higher than what is considered safe. A short time later, her twelve-year-old daughter began to lose her balance and fall over while walking. Although the energy company that dug the natural gas well denied that fracking was responsible for these health problems, the family was not convinced. They packed their belongings and moved away from the area to escape the effects of water pollution.

John Barnes. "Harrowing Experience with Niece's Health." West Virginia for Moratorium on Marcellus (blog), September 16, 2011. http://wv4mom.org/content/harrowing-experience-nieces-health.

Health Effects of Water Pollution

The various types of water pollutants all have different effects on human health and the environment. Whether a certain pollutant is harmful depends on many factors, including its concentration, the timing of its release, the size and composition of the body of water it enters, and the organisms that live in or use that water. Discharges from point sources are usually easier to monitor and regulate than nonpoint source pollution, or runoff. In some cases, water pollution from runoff makes lakes and rivers unsafe for people to use, resulting in beaches being closed and residents being warned to boil their drinking water.

One of the effects of nutrient pollution is eutrophication, which can result in harmful algal blooms (HABs). Algae are tiny, single-celled organisms that live in water. They are not harmful in small quantities, but nutrients like nitrogen and phosphorus cause them to grow rapidly and produce toxins. These toxins can be dangerous to people or animals who drink or swim in the water. Some of the health risks associated with HABs include skin rashes, stomach and liver problems, respiratory problems, and neurological problems. Nitrogen in drinking water also causes a condition called "blue baby syndrome," in which infants who consume contaminated water have trouble breathing and develop a blue tinge to their skin and lips.

Toxic chemicals used to control pests can enter both surface water and groundwater through runoff. The main health

A woman displays the lesions that developed on her feet as a result of using arsenic-contaminated drinking water. Water contaminated with heavy metals can cause serious health consequences.

risks associated with pesticides in water supplies come from drinking contaminated water or eating seafood from contaminated water. The EPA, WHO, and other organizations have established guidelines to let people know how much pesticide residue they can safely consume. Going beyond the acceptable levels of consumption can cause serious health effects, including cancer, tumors, reproductive problems, immune system failure, hormone disruption, cellular damage, physical deformities, and even death.

Heavy metals have some of the most serious health effects of all the types of water pollutants. Lead, which can enter water through industrial pollution or the erosion of old pipes, is particularly dangerous to children. An estimated 250,000 American children are exposed to levels of lead that have the potential to harm their physical and mental development. Some of the health risks associated with lead exposure include anemia, brittle bones, and nervous system damage. Arsenic is another metal contaminant that is poisonous in drinking water. It can cause skin discoloration and lesions, tingling and weakness in the limbs, nausea, cancer, or death.

Mercury is a heavy metal water pollutant that contaminates fish, making them dangerous for people to eat—especially children and pregnant women—due to the risk of neurological disorders and birth defects. The EPA conducts surveys of the amount of mercury found in various bodies of water and issues consumption advisories for different species of fish. Some of the fish highest in mercury are large predator species like shark, swordfish, marlin, orange roughy, king mackerel, and ahi tuna. Rich Gelfond, an executive for the film-technology company Imax, was an avid runner and tennis player until he began feeling dizzy all the time and experiencing numbness in his feet and tremors in his hands. Finally, after learning that Gelfond ate sushi made from tuna and swordfish every day, a doctor diagnosed him with mercury poisoning. "I was just so frustrated that I was trying to do something good for my body and in fact I was poisoning myself,"[9] he said.

Pathogens pose a serious health risk for humans, especially in developing countries. Studies have shown that

THE CONNECTION BETWEEN POLLUTION AND DISEASE

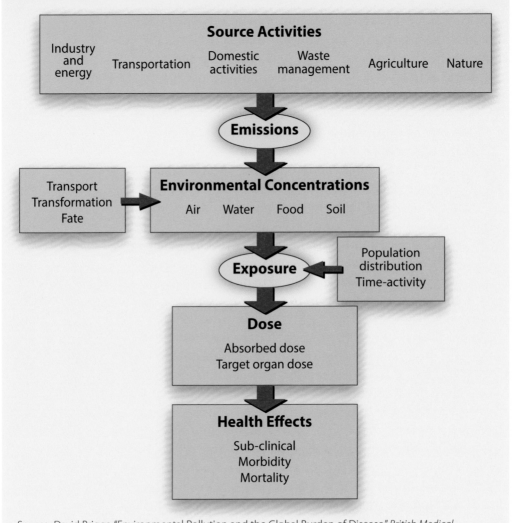

Source Activities

Industry and energy   Transportation   Domestic activities   Waste management   Agriculture   Nature

Emissions

Transport Transformation Fate

Environmental Concentrations

Air   Water   Food   Soil

Exposure

Population distribution Time-activity

Dose

Absorbed dose
Target organ dose

Health Effects

Sub-clinical
Morbidity
Mortality

Source: David Briggs. "Environmental Pollution and the Global Burden of Disease." *British Medical Bulletin*, vol. 68, no. 1, pp. 1–24. http://bmb.oxfordjournals.org/content/68/1/1.full.

40 percent of the world's population lives in places that lack good sanitation. In these places, the available freshwater is often contaminated with human or animal waste. These waste products contain harmful bacteria and viruses that can cause serious gastrointestinal illnesses. Bacteria like *E. coli*

cause diarrhea and vomiting, while protozoans like *Giardia* cause diarrhea and severe stomach cramps. Without access to clean water for drinking and basic hygiene, more than 2 million people die from diarrhea each year.

Hydrocarbon water pollution often comes from spills or seepage of fuels, solvents, or chemicals like tetrachloroethylene, which is commonly used in dry cleaning. Oil spills pose a serious risk to the environment as well as to human health. When the oil tanker *Exxon Valdez* crashed into a reef and dumped half a million barrels of oil into the Gulf of Alaska in 1989, for instance, it resulted in the death of 250,000 seabirds, 2,800 otters, 300 harbor seals, 250 bald eagles, and 22 whales. Commercial fisherman Bob Linville participated in efforts to contain the oil spill and clean up beaches in Prince William Sound. He blames his exposure to the crude oil and chemicals used to disperse it for mysterious, chronic health problems he has experienced in the decades since then. "I got what turned out to be an autoimmune disease," he explained. "Eventually my bone marrow failed, I got aplastic anemia, I had two or three other complications. Really, it was like sixteen years of illness for me, physically."[10]

Water Pollution Control Laws and Strategies

The passage of the Clean Water Act (CWA; originally known as the Federal Water Pollution Control Act) in 1972 marked the point when the U.S. government started to crack down on point source effluent releases. Up to that time, cities and industries dumped chemicals and sewage into American waterways almost without regulation or consequences, and this practice took a terrible toll on water quality. In 1969—the year the Cuyahoga River fire caught public attention—99 percent of fish sampled in Chesapeake Bay contained DDT, bacteria levels in the Hudson River were 170 times higher than considered safe, and tests showed that 30 percent of U.S. drinking water contained dangerous chemicals.

The goal of the CWA was to "restore and maintain the

chemical, physical, and biological integrity of our nation's waters." The CWA established the basic legal structure for regulating pollutant discharges into American surface waters. It gave the EPA the authority to set water quality standards for various pollutants, establish pollution control requirements for industry, and help cities build or upgrade sewage treatment plants. Under CWA provisions, it was against the law to discharge any regulated pollutant into the water without an EPA permit.

The CWA made a tremendous impact on point sources of pollution, greatly reducing the effluent discharges from factories, sewage treatment plants, and other facilities. In the decades since its passage, the number of lakes and rivers that meet water quality standards has doubled, and many urban waterways that were once heavily polluted have become clean, inviting centerpieces of cities' renewal efforts. For all its successes, however, the CWA did not address nonpoint sources of pollution, so runoff from city streets and farm fields remains a problem. One dire example is the Mississippi River, which picks up nutrient pollution throughout its huge drainage area and deposits it into the Gulf of Mexico. These nutrients cause eutrophication in the warm waters of the Gulf, which creates an oxygen-starved "dead zone" that grows to 5,000 square miles (13,000 sq. km) or more—about the size of Connecticut—every summer.

Although Congress has expanded the CWA with amendments several times, the U.S. Supreme Court has also narrowed its scope. A 2001 ruling, for instance, said that states could not use the CWA to protect isolated wetlands from development. Finally, up to 100,000 violations of the CWA occur each year, ranging from small, accidental spills to large-scale, illegal dumping of toxins. In 2000, for example, a Massey Energy impoundment broke in Martin County, Kentucky, releasing 300 million gallons (1.1 billion L) of coal slurry. The toxic sludge buried local homes and yards up to 7 feet (2.1m) deep, killed all the fish in two nearby streams,

and polluted 60 miles (97km) of river that supplied drinking water to area residents.

Since the CWA does not cover underground water supplies, Congress passed the Safe Drinking Water Act (SDWA) in 1974. This legislation authorized the EPA to set health-based standards for drinking water and regulate 160,000 public water systems nationwide. The SDWA is intended to protect public health by monitoring both naturally occurring and man-made contaminants that may be found in drinking water. It does not cover private wells that serve fewer than twenty-five people, and it does not apply to bottled water.

The SDWA has helped to make American drinking water some of the safest in the world. "Safe, clean water is the first line of defense in protecting public health, protecting our children and our families, and protecting the basic values that are fundamental to the American quality of life,"[11] declared former vice president Al Gore. Since its passage,

A cleanup crew works to clear a driveway inundated in coal slurry after the sludge pond broke at a nearby mine in Martin County, Kentucky, in 2000.

however, more than 2,000 contaminants have been found in American drinking water, and nearly 200 of those have been found to have dangerous health effects at certain levels. Drinking water also faces new threats from energy production techniques like hydraulic fracturing (fracking), which pump toxic chemicals underground, and overuse for irrigation of crops in dry regions, which causes groundwater to become increasingly salty (salinity).

The diverse threats to water quality in the twenty-first century are complicated to identify and regulate. "When we started regulating water pollution in the 1970s, there was a huge public outcry because you could see raw sewage flowing into the rivers," said former EPA director William D. Ruckelshaus. "Today the violations are much more subtle—pesticides and chemicals you can't see or smell that are even more dangerous. . . . And so a lot of the public pressure on regulatory agencies has ebbed away."[12]

CHAPTER 3

Hazardous Chemicals and Health

Everything in the physical world is made up of chemicals, from water and food to animals and humans. Thousands of different chemicals occur naturally in the environment, and thousands of others are produced through human industry. Although many chemicals can be harmful, especially in large doses, many others offer health benefits or serve other important uses. Chlorine, for instance, is helpful when it is used to disinfect swimming pools and drinking water, whiten clothing and paper, or extinguish fires. Some examples of helpful applications of man-made chemicals include medicines to prevent and treat diseases, fertilizers to help farmers produce more food, preservatives to make food last longer, pesticides to kill harmful insects, detergents to clean clothes and sterilize dishes, antifreeze to help car engines withstand extreme temperatures, synthetic fibers to keep athletes warm and dry, and plastics to create toys, electronics, and countless other consumer products.

Thanks to the usefulness of chemicals, the U.S. chemical industry grew rapidly during the twentieth century. By 2012 it earned an estimated $770 billion, employed more than eight hundred thousand people, and supplied a wide variety of chemicals to nearly every other major industry

While hazardous chemicals have many important uses, they can pose a serious risk to human health and the environment when used or disposed of improperly.

around the world. But the production, usage, and disposal of chemicals can be dangerous to human health and to the environment. Many chemicals that are beneficial in small amounts can be toxic in larger amounts, and some chemicals that are harmless alone can be toxic in combination with other chemicals. Although chlorine has many useful applications, for example, it is also a key ingredient in a number of chemicals that are considered hazardous pollutants, such as chlorofluorocarbons (CFCs), dichlorodiphenyltrichloroethane (DDT), and polychlorinated biphenyls (PCBs). In addition, many useful chemicals are not biodegradable, so they do not break down when they enter the environment. Instead, they build up to hazardous levels over time. These factors make it very difficult to handle and dispose of chemicals safely. When chemicals are spilled or disposed of improperly in toxic waste sites, they pollute the air, water, and soil and pose a serious risk to humans and ecosystems.

Raising Awareness of Hazardous Chemicals

Until the 1960s, few people questioned the safety of the chemicals that promised to make their lives easier and more comfortable. One commonly used chemical was the pesticide DDT, which was sprayed on farm fields and neighborhoods across the country to kill mosquitoes and other insects. But in 1962, biologist and nature writer Rachel Carson published *Silent Spring*, a book that documented the health risks and environmental damage—especially declining bird populations—caused by the indiscriminate use of pesticides and other toxic chemicals. "We have allowed these chemicals to be used with little or no advance investigation of their effect on soil, water, wildlife, and man himself," Carson wrote. "Future generations are unlikely to condone our lack of prudent concern for the integrity of the natural world that supports all life."[13] Carson's book, and the resulting public outcry, led the U.S. government to establish the Environmental Protection Agency (EPA) and ban the use of DDT.

Around the same time, people around the world grew concerned about the safety of pharmaceutical drugs. A drug called thalidomide was developed in Germany and promoted across Europe as a miracle cure for everything from anxiety and insomnia to coughs and headaches. Many pregnant women took it to relieve the symptoms of morning sickness, but it turned out that thalidomide had terrible effects on developing babies in the womb. An estimated 10,000 babies whose mothers took thalidomide were born with severe limb deformities and other birth defects, and more than 2,000 of them died. The scandal surrounding "thalidomide babies" forced the drug company to take the medicine off the market, and it also prompted the U.S. government to grant the Food and Drug Administration (FDA) increased authority to ensure the safety of pharmaceutical products.

The health risks associated with chemicals returned to the news in 1978 with the discovery of a toxic waste site at Love Canal, a working-class community near Niagara Falls, New York. Over the course of thirty years, the Hooker Chemical

Company dumped 21,000 tons (19,000t) of toxic chemical waste into a partially completed canal near the Niagara River. In 1953, the company covered the dump site with dirt and sold the property to a developer. The Love Canal neighborhood, consisting of eight hundred homes and a school, soon rose up on the site. Few people worried about the safety of the community until 1978, when record rainfall in the area caused long-buried toxic chemicals to percolate upward

Activist Lois Gibbs speaks at an event commemorating the twenty-fifth anniversary of the 1978 evacuation of the Love Canal neighborhood in Niagara Falls, New York. Gibbs led successful efforts to investigate health problems in the community caused by toxic waste from a chemical plant.

through the soil and leach into basements and underground water supplies. "We knew they put chemicals into the canal and filled it over," said one longtime resident, "but we had no idea the chemicals would invade our homes. We're worried sick about the grandchildren and their children."[14]

Unfortunately, Love Canal residents had reason to be concerned. The seeping chemicals caused trees, grass, and gardens to turn black and die. Children who jumped in puddles on the school playground came home with chemical burns. People were shocked to learn that the soil and water in the neighborhood contained eighty-two different chemical compounds—eleven of which were known to cause cancer, including benzene and dioxin. Surveys revealed that Love Canal residents suffered high incidences of a number of health problems, such as asthma, epilepsy, and leukemia. In addition, 56 percent of the children born to families living in Love Canal between 1974 and 1978 had at least one birth defect.

After local mother Lois Gibbs rallied Love Canal residents and other concerned citizens in protest, the federal government purchased all the homes in the neighborhood and relocated the families. New York State health commissioner David Axelrod declared that the Love Canal tragedy served as a "national symbol of a failure to exercise a sense of concern for future generations."[15] Congress responded in 1980 by passing the Comprehensive Environmental Response, Compensation, and Liability Act (CERCLA), more commonly known as the Superfund Act. Superfund established a program to identify and clean up abandoned toxic waste sites. It also gave the EPA the power to force those responsible for creating the waste to cover the costs of cleanup. Under Superfund, the EPA identified more than thirty thousand potential hazardous waste sites across the United States.

Sources of Hazardous Chemicals

The chemical manufacturing industry is the source of most hazardous chemicals. Centered mainly in the United States, Europe, and Japan, it takes raw materials that occur in nature and converts them into other compounds. Between

The Bhopal Chemical Spill

One of the worst disasters involving toxic chemicals occurred in Bhopal, India, in 1984. Late one night, a Union Carbide Corporation chemical plant leaked 27 tons (24.5t) of methyl isocyanate (MIC), a hazardous chemical used in the production of pesticides. Toxic fumes settled in a dense cloud over the heavily populated city. People who inhaled the poison gas had trouble breathing, coughed violently, vomited uncontrollably, and went into convulsions. "It felt like somebody had filled our bodies up with red chilis, our eyes had tears coming out, noses were watering, we had froth in our mouths," survivor Champa Devi Shukla remembers. "The coughing was so bad that people were writhing in pain."

Many people left their homes and ran through the streets in a desperate attempt to escape the fumes. "Some people just got up and ran in whatever they were wearing or even if they were wearing nothing at all," Shukla recalls. "Those who fell were not picked up by anybody, they just kept falling, and were trampled on by other people. People climbed and scrambled over each other to save their lives." An estimated 4,000 people died that night, and more than 20,000 others succumbed over the next few weeks. Even fifteen years later, tests showed levels of toxic chemicals in Bhopal's groundwater from 20,000 to 6,000,000 times higher than considered safe. Residents of the city continue to suffer high rates of birth defects, cancer, and respiratory disorders.

"What Happened?" Bhopal Medical Appeal, 2014. www.bhopal.org/what-happened.

70,000 and 80,000 different chemical compounds are produced and used regularly around the world. The primary industrial users of these chemicals include textile and apparel makers, pulp and paper companies, petroleum refiners, and manufacturers of rubber and plastic products. Some chemicals, like fertilizers and pesticides, are introduced into the environment on purpose in order to provide a certain benefit. Other chemicals enter the environment as byproducts of industrial processes, through accidental spills and releases, or through improper disposal.

Types of Hazardous Chemicals

Chemicals can be hazardous in four main ways. They can be corrosive, meaning that they burn through or eat away containers and other things that they contact; ignitable, meaning that they catch on fire easily; reactive, meaning that they become poisonous or explosive when they combine with other chemicals; or toxic, meaning that they are poisonous to humans and other living creatures in certain amounts or through certain types of exposure. Toxic chemicals have other traits that make them particularly hazardous. Many toxins do not break down in the environment or dissolve in water, so they tend to remain in the fatty tissues of animals that are exposed to them. As these animals are consumed by other animals or humans, the toxins can bioaccumulate, or build up to higher and higher concentrations as they make their way up the food chain.

Toxic chemicals that remain in the environment and bioaccumulate are known as persistent organic pollutants (POPs). The twelve most hazardous POPs—known as the "dirty dozen"—received special mention from the United Nations in the Stockholm Convention of 2001. This treaty, which was signed by more than 150 countries, was intended to eliminate the production and usage of the listed POPs and to ensure the safe disposal of those already in existence. The original twelve chemicals were aldrin, chlordane, DDT, dieldrin, dibenzofurans, dioxins, endrin, heptachlor, hexachlorobenzene (HCB), Mirex, PCBs, and toxaphene. Several additional chemicals have been added over the years.

Although DDT appears on the list of POPs and has been banned in the United States and most other developed

NUTRITION FACT

34,000

The number of cancer deaths per year that can be directly linked to environmental exposures to specific, known carcinogenic substances countries, the pesticide remains in use in Africa and other developing areas of the world. Despite the risks to wildlife and ecosystems, DDT is highly effective in reducing the population of mosquitoes that carry malaria. This deadly disease kills millions of people each year in tropical regions of the world, so some argue that the benefits of using DDT outweigh the risks.

Dioxins are a family of toxic chemical compounds that are formed in many different industrial processes. They are created in the manufacture of pesticides and herbicides, for example, and they are also released in the combustion of coal, diesel fuel, treated wood, or garbage. Although the health effects of some dioxins are not well known, others have proved to be very dangerous. Agent Orange is a chemical herbicide that contains dioxins and other toxins. The U.S. military used 20 million gallons (76 million L) of it during the Vietnam War to kill jungle vegetation that provided hiding places for enemy troops. Later research found high rates of cancer and nerve, skin, and respiratory disorders among

A man fumigates with DDT to control against mosquitos in Mamallapuram, India. While banned in most developed countries, DDT is still used for mosquito and pest control in many developing nations.

Contamination in "Nature's First Food"

"In this jar is the most highly chemically-contaminated human food on the planet," scientist and environmental activist Sandra Steingraber stated in the documentary film *Living Downstream*. "It has more dioxins, more toilet deodorizers, more mothproofing agents, dry cleaning fluid, pesticides, and PCBs than any other human food." The jar that Steingraber was holding contained breast milk from a nursing mother.

Human breast milk contains about 3 percent fat. In producing milk, a woman's body draws from all of its fat reserves. But many of the persistent organic pollutants (POPs) found in the environment are lipophilic, or fat soluble, meaning that they dissolve in fat rather than water. These sorts of chemicals can remain in the environment for decades, and they end up being stored in the fatty tissues of people who are exposed to them. As a result, nearly all breast milk contains some toxic chemical contaminants. As Steingraber pointed out, these chemicals "didn't get there on purpose. They were carried to us by ecological forces outside of our individual control. They represent a form of toxic trespass."

Although the effects of these chemicals on developing babies have not been fully investigated, pediatricians still insist that breastfeeding offers many health benefits that make it the best choice for an infant's first six months of life. They say that the level of contaminants in breast milk is likely to be low unless the mother is exposed to exceptional amounts of chemicals at home, in the workplace, or through her diet.

Bill Moyers. "Sandra Steingraber's War on Toxic Trespassers." *Moyers and Company*, April 19, 2013. http://billmoyers.com/segment/sandra-steingrabers-war-on-toxic-trespassers.

American servicemen who were exposed to the chemical. Millions of Vietnamese also experienced health problems associated with Agent Orange, and high levels of dioxins are still present in the nation's soil and water.

PCBs are persistent organic pollutants that were used extensively in electrical insulation and in paints, cements, adhesives, and hydraulic fluids until they were banned in the United States in 1977. Since they remain in the environment for long periods of time, PCBs still contaminate many bodies of water—such as the Great Lakes and the Hudson River—as well as the soil around many landfills and former production and storage facilities.

In addition to POPs, many other chemicals cause concern because they are commonly found in consumer products. Bisphenol A (BPA) is a chemical frequently used in plastic products to make them strong, lightweight, and resistant to heat and odors. When it is used in food containers like baby bottles, however, BPA can leach out of the plastic and enter the food. Once it enters the human body, BPA acts like a synthetic hormone and creates health risks associated with growth and reproductive systems. Brominated flame retardants (BFRs) are chemicals added to goods like bedding, pajamas, furniture, and carpeting to prevent them from burning. Since exposure to the chemical may affect growth and development, many countries have banned their use in products used by children. Perfluorinated compounds (PFCs) are chemicals used in nonstick cookware and water-resistant clothing. PFCs have been linked to health risks such as birth defects, developmental disorders, and cancer.

Health Effects of Exposure to Chemicals

People can be exposed to hazardous chemicals in the environment by inhaling polluted air, drinking polluted water, eating contaminated food, or contacting contaminated soil with their skin. The health risks associated with exposure depend on the type of chemical, the amount or concentration, the timing of the exposure, and the person's overall "body burden," or accumulation of toxic chemicals in the body over time. Children are much more vulnerable to the effects of toxic chemical exposure than adults. Children spend more time on the ground, so they absorb more chemicals through their skin. Children also breathe more rapidly, eat more food in relation to their body weight, and take longer to digest food—all of which lead to increased exposure to chemicals. Finally, children are growing and developing, so chemicals that enter their bodies are more likely to have harmful health effects.

Although thousands of different chemicals are produced every day—and used in everything from body lotion and nail polish to oven cleaners and plastic wrap—little information is available regarding the health effects and safe levels of exposure for many of these compounds. Consumer advocates argue that every chemical should be tested extensively and proved to be safe before it is used in commercial applications and people are exposed to it. In reality, though, this rarely happens. Most research into the harmful effects of chemicals is conducted on animals, and the results do not always apply to humans in the same way. Some chemicals may appear to be safe in initial tests but later end up causing problems in high doses, in combination with other chemicals, or through repeated exposure. In many cases, health effects only begin to appear after a chemical has been in widespread use. "We are, by default, conducting a massive

People come into contact with thousands of chemical compounds in everyday products, but the health effects from and safe levels of exposure for many chemicals is unknown.

clinical toxicology trial, and our children and their children are the experimental animals,"[16] according to Herbert L. Needleman in *Raising Children Toxic Free*. Even when people experience health problems after being exposed to a certain chemical, however, it is often difficult to prove a direct cause-and-effect relationship.

Despite the lack of direct evidence, researchers suspect that many everyday chemicals do affect human health. Some scientists believe that toxic chemicals in the air, water, food, and soil have contributed to an overall increase in allergies, asthma, and diabetes in the United States during the twenty-first century. Studies have also shown that people who are consistently exposed to low doses of pesticides over long periods of time—like farmers—have a 70 percent higher risk of developing Parkinson's disease. People who were exposed to Agent Orange during the Vietnam War have reported a range of health problems, including prostate cancer, lung cancers, Hodgkin's disease, and children born with developmental disorders and mutations.

Many of the chemicals that cause the most human health concern—including DDT and other pesticides, dioxins, PCBs, bisphenol A, and phthalates (chemicals found in soft plastics and vinyl products)—are known as endocrine disruptors. The endocrine system controls the production of hormones that regulate important bodily functions, such as growth, metabolism, and sexual development. Endocrine disruptors interfere with or block the action of natural hormones, which may lead to serious health issues. These chemicals are found in many common household products, including food containers, toys, clothing, and cosmetics. Exposure to endocrine disruptors is especially dangerous for pregnant women, nursing mothers, and infants because they may contribute to birth defects, genital abnormalities, developmental delays, behavioral problems, and immune system dysfunction. Some scientists also point to endocrine disruptors as the cause of earlier puberty in American girls. Studies have shown that the average age at the onset of puberty has dropped from eleven to nine since the 1960s. Early puberty increases girls' risk of obesity and reproductive cancers later in life.

THE GREENPEACE PYRAMID OF PLASTICS

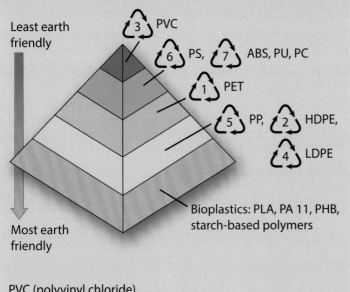

Least earth friendly

3 PVC

6 PS, 7 ABS, PU, PC

1 PET

5 PP, 2 HDPE,

4 LDPE

Bioplastics: PLA, PA 11, PHB, starch-based polymers

Most earth friendly

PVC (polyvinyl chloride)

PS (polystyrene); other resins such as ABS (acrylonitrile butadine styrene); PU (polyurethane); PC (polycarbonate)

PET (polyethylene terephthalate)

PP (polypropylene); HDPE (high-density polyethylene); LDPE (low-density polyethylene)

Bioplastics: PLA (polylactide acid), PA 11 (Polyamide 11), PHB (Poly 3 hydroxybutyrate)

Source: Adapted from www.greenpeace.org.

Laws and Strategies for Dealing with Hazardous Chemicals

In the United States, a number of different government agencies take part in protecting citizens from exposure to hazardous chemicals. The US Food and Drug

Administration (FDA) regulates food products, cosmetics, and pharmaceutical drugs that are sold in the United States. Although the FDA requires medicines to undergo rigorous testing before they are approved for use, cosmetics, nutritional supplements, and food packaging are not closely monitored. The Consumer Product Safety Commission is in charge of ensuring the safety of goods sold to American consumers. The agency occasionally takes steps to prevent the use of toxic chemicals in items that are likely to be handled by children. It banned the use of fire resistant chemi-

Giant, mountain-sized piles of discarded rock from the Tar Creek mine leach heavy metals into the groundwater of the now-deserted town of Picher, Oklahoma—one of the most toxic areas in the United States.

cals known as Tris in car seats, changing table pads, and other baby furniture, for instance, and it asked manufacturers to remove phthalates from chewable toys.

The main U.S. law intended to protect citizens from hazardous chemicals is the Toxic Substances Control Act (TSCA). Passed by Congress in 1976, the TSCA gave the EPA authority to review new and existing chemicals to ensure that they are safe. Shortly after launching its review process, the EPA banned the production and use of PCBs. The agency also banned the pesticide chlordane in 1988 after it was linked to respiratory problems, neurological disorders, and some forms of cancer. Despite these actions, however, the TSCA has come under heavy criticism from environmental groups and consumer advocates. They claim that the law is weak, outdated, and ineffective in protecting Americans from exposure to dangerous chemicals.

Critics argue that the TSCA allows manufacturers to put hazardous chemicals in common household products without requiring safety tests. They also say that the law makes it nearly impossible for the EPA to restrict the use of such chemicals or remove them from the market—even when studies indicate that the chemicals may cause cancer or other serious health effects. In order to regulate a chemical, the EPA must prove that it poses an "unreasonable risk" to public health or the environment.

In the decades since the TSCA was passed, the EPA has only thoroughly tested about 200 chemicals and regulated the use of five. This means that 62,000 chemicals introduced before 1976 remained on the market without testing, and 22,000 chemicals developed since that time have never been fully assessed for toxic impacts on human health and the environment. "[Are chemicals] innocent until proven guilty? Are they allowed on the market first until we can prove by dying or by harmed children that the chemicals should not be on the market?" scientist and environmental activist Sandra Steingraber asked. "Or are we going to . . . say that before a chemical can be marketed you have to demonstrate through careful testing that almost certainly no one is going to get hurt? Most people would agree that the second way of doing things is the ethical, rational way to go forward and a lot of people are surprised to learn that that's not how we do things in the United States."[17]

Environmental groups have proposed a number of revisions and updates to the law to give the EPA more power to test and regulate chemicals before they appear in consumer products. Some of these proposed changes are modeled on the program for Registration, Evaluation, Authorisation, and Restriction of Chemicals (REACH) adopted in Europe in 2006. REACH requires chemical manufacturers to test and provide safety information about their products before they can be used in consumer goods. The program also works toward phasing out hazardous chemicals already in use and finding safer alternatives. Finally, REACH provides citizens with information about the chemicals present in the products they use to help them make decisions about their own health and safety.

Although REACH serves to protect people from chemicals currently in use, some people are harmed by toxic chemicals that entered the environment long ago. In the United States, the Superfund Act of 1980 authorized the EPA to locate toxic waste disposal sites, track down the responsible parties, and force them to pay to clean up the contamination. Once a site is proposed as a potential Superfund site, the EPA and state authorities conduct an assessment and give it a score using the Hazard Ranking System. A score of 28.5 points or above (on a scale from 1 to 100) means that the site is placed on the National Priorities List for eventual cleanup.

As of 2014 the National Priorities List included 1,322 sites in various stages of cleanup. According to the EPA, this means that half of all Americans live within 10 miles (16km) of a Superfund site. A total of 384 sites have been cleaned up enough to be deleted from the list since the program started, and about 70 percent of the cleanup costs have been paid by the responsible parties. Cleaning up a Superfund site can be very time-consuming and expensive. At the Tar Creek mine site in Oklahoma, for instance, the cleanup process has taken twenty years and cost $100 million, yet the site is still contaminated with unsafe levels of lead, zinc, and cadmium.

As the number of Superfund sites shows, safe, long-term disposal of hazardous chemicals can be difficult to accomplish. Some common disposal methods for toxins include burying them in secure landfills, burning them at high temperatures, pumping them into deep underground wells, and impounding them in lined ponds. All of these methods, however, have the potential to allow the chemicals to escape and contaminate the air, water, and soil. Environmental activists argue that the best approach to ensuring the health of future generations is to reduce the production and use of hazardous chemicals and develop safer alternatives.

CHAPTER 4

Other Types of Pollution and Health

I n addition to the many chemicals and other substances that pollute the air, water, and soil, energy can also be a pollutant. Whether it takes the form of noise, light, heat, or radiation, energy has the potential to disrupt the functioning of the natural environment and cause harmful effects to human health. Another troublesome type of pollution is municipal solid waste—more commonly known as garbage. Americans generate 251 million tons (228 million t) of garbage per year, or an average of 4.38 pounds (2kg) per person per day. Disposing of this huge amount of trash creates many challenges. The majority ends up in landfills or incinerators, causing air, water, and soil pollution as well as producing methane gas that contributes to global climate change.

Noise Pollution and Health

Excessive, loud, or unpleasant noise is considered an environmental pollutant. The main sources of noise pollution include industrial machinery, construction equipment, automobile traffic, trains and airplanes, social and sporting events, lawn services, and household appliances. Poor urban planning is a major contributing factor to noise pol-

Construction sites are one of many sources of noise pollution in urban areas. The loud machinery also puts workers on those sites at a higher risk for hearing loss.

lution, as crowded living conditions and congested streets create many loud sounds.

Noise pollution is not only annoying to people who are exposed to it, but it also has the potential to harm their physical and mental health. "Calling noise a nuisance is like calling smog an inconvenience," said former U.S. surgeon general William H. Stewart. "Noise must be considered a hazard to the health of people everywhere."[18]

Exposure to loud noises can cause serious damage to a person's sense of hearing. Any sound with a volume of 90 decibels or more can cause temporary or partial hearing loss, while sounds with a volume of 120 decibels or more can cause permanent hearing damage. Loud noises thus pose a major health risk for people in certain occupations, such as mining, factory work, construction, or rock music.

Excessive noise levels are also linked to other health problems, including sleep disorders, fatigue, stress, irritability, aggressive behavior, and headaches. Constant exposure to unpleasant sounds has been shown to contribute to chronic health conditions like high blood pressure and cardiovascular disease. These issues often affect people who live near airports, train tracks, or busy highways.

Noise pollution also has negative effects on the environment. Animals have more sensitive ears than humans, and many species depend on their hearing for survival. When wild animals are exposed to loud noises and experience hearing loss, they may be unable to hunt for food or to avoid predators. Hearing loss can also prevent animals from responding to mating calls, which can cause a decline in population. Some species depend on sound to provide cues for migration or nighttime navigation, so loud noise or hearing loss can cause them to become disoriented or lost. Some studies show that animals are becoming louder in order to adapt to the higher sound levels in the environment, which further increases noise pollution.

The main U.S. law dealing with noise pollution is the Noise Control Act of 1972, which gave the Environmental Protection Agency (EPA) authority to establish standards for various sources of noise. Although Congress ended funding for the law in 1981, state and local governments have continued to pass noise ordinances and take noise control into account in urban planning decisions. Other possible approaches to reducing noise pollution include developing quieter engines and equipment, improving roads and traf-

Underwater Noise Pollution

Water pollution is not the only concern for animals that live in the ocean. They also are affected by increasing levels of underwater noise pollution. Offshore oil drilling, transoceanic shipping, sonar employed by military vessels and commercial fishing fleets, and other human activities all generate loud noises in the world's oceans. Since sound travels much farther and faster in water than it does in air, these noises carry for thousands of miles underwater.

Many species of marine mammals depend on sound to communicate, and underwater noise pollution makes it difficult for them to hear mating calls or warning signals. Some species, like dolphins and porpoises, use sounds bouncing off objects (known as echolocation) to help them navigate and locate prey. In addition to disrupting these basic behaviors, loud noises in the ocean can also frighten or disorient marine life—sometimes with deadly consequences. Studies have linked mass strandings of whales on beaches to seismic surveys of the ocean floor by the oil industry. Conducting these surveys involves shooting blasts of sound louder than a jet engine several times per minute.

Some steps are being taken to reduce the impact of noise pollution on marine life. The International Maritime Organization, which is responsible for ocean safety worldwide, established guidelines to reduce noise levels of commercial ships. In addition, scientists have mapped key migration routes and feeding areas and encouraged ships performing oil exploration and military testing to avoid those areas. Still, marine biologists worry about the long-term health effects of loud ocean noises on marine life.

fic control, removing public loudspeakers, controlling the sound levels in bars and nightclubs, and lowering the volume of stereos and televisions in homes.

Light Pollution and Health

Light is another form of energy that can be considered an environmental pollutant. Although artificial light is integral to modern life and offers many benefits, bad lighting design allows too much light to shine where it is not needed. This light pollution removes the darkness from the night sky and affects the light/dark cycles of the natural world.

Two-thirds of Americans, and one-fifth of all people worldwide, live in areas with so much artificial illumination that the Milky Way is not visible in the night sky.

Exposure to excessive artificial light alters the biological rhythms of human beings and many other species. Darkness provides an important cue to tell the body's internal clock that it is time to sleep. Artificial light extends the daytime and shortens the night, reducing the number of hours people devote to rest. The biological consequences of sleep deprivation include fatigue, irritability, and poor concentration. In addition, studies have found a correlation between exposure to nighttime brightness and breast cancer in women. Researchers note that light reduces the production of melatonin, a hormone secreted at night that helps balance reproductive hormones and suppress tumor formation.

Light pollution also impacts the behavior and health of many animal species. It disrupts bird migration, sea turtle nesting, sockeye salmon spawning, and nighttime feeding by bats, owls, and other nocturnal animals. "We know enough now that we can say anytime we spill light into the sky, we're

Dim the Lights, See the Stars

On satellite images of the earth at night, it is easy to see the major cities, which look like bright bulbs on a string of white Christmas lights. To people on the ground, the bright city lights have the opposite effect—they make it almost impossible to see the stars in the night sky. In fact, many city dwellers have never experienced a starry night. When Los Angeles had a major blackout in 1994, some residents were so shocked by the sight of thousands of points of light in the sky that they called a local observatory to find out what was happening.

Some cities have responded to the problem of light pollution by passing ordinances to regulate the use of outdoor lighting at night. Dripping Springs, Texas, for instance, limits the total amount of lighting that a home or business can use and requires all lights to be shielded. People whose lights shine beyond their own property can be fined for trespassing under the law. These measures helped Dripping Springs become the first city in Texas, and only the sixth in the world, to be recognized as an International Dark Sky Community.

Some people believe that outdoor lighting is harmless and only adds to the safety and convenience of modern life. But many others cherish the ability to connect with the cosmos. "What are we losing by not being able to see the starry skies?" asked astronomer Bill Wren. "I think there are significant consequences. Imagining worlds beyond our own horizon, just that cognitive ability. How do you expect the kids to reach for the stars if they can't see them?"

Forrest Wilder. "Seeing Stars in Dripping Springs." *Texas Observer*, May 20, 2014. http://www.texasobserver.org /seeing-stars-dripping-springs-light-pollution/.

putting animals and wildlife at risk, and we're probably putting ourselves at risk,"[19] said Chad Moore, manager of the night skies program for the U.S. National Park Service.

Although it is not practical or desirable to get rid of all artificial light, there are many steps that can reduce harmful light pollution. Studies show that as much as half of all the light projected at night is wasted, so a simple solution is to turn off lights when they are not needed. Changes in lighting design can redirect light downward to illuminate streets and sidewalks, and installing motion sensors and automatic cutoffs can help limit light use. Many cities and even some countries have adopted strict regulations to control light pollution. Flagstaff, Arizona, was declared the nation's first International Dark Sky Community in 2001, and many International Dark Sky Parks and Reserves have been created around the world since then.

Thermal Pollution and Health

Heat is another form of energy that can become a pollutant in certain circumstances. Thermal pollution occurs when heat that is introduced into the environment causes the natural temperature to change. Most harmful thermal pollution affects bodies of water. Although it is sometimes produced by natural sources like lightning, geothermal hot springs, or volcanic eruptions, it is usually caused by human activity. Electrical power plants and industrial factories, for instance, often draw water from natural sources and use it to cool machinery. When this water is released back into the environment with a higher temperature, it reduces the oxygen level of the water in the lake or stream, which can harm marine life and destroy ecosystems.

Development and construction along the shorelines of lakes and rivers also contribute to thermal pollution. Trees and plants along the water's edge shade lakes and rivers from direct sunlight and help moderate the water temperature. Removing vegetation for development not only makes the water absorb more heat, but it also causes soil erosion along the banks. The sediments reduce oxygen levels in the water and promote the growth of harmful algae. When areas near natural bodies of water are paved over to create roads, parking lots, and driveways, these impervious surfaces cause rain to flow directly into lakes and streams. Since paved surfaces tend to retain heat, this warm runoff increases the water temperature.

Thermal pollution can thus take a serious toll on the environment. By decreasing oxygen levels in lakes and rivers, thermal pollution promotes harmful algae growth and suffocates fish and amphibians. Thermal pollution can also disrupt the function of natural ecosystems, causing native species to die off and allowing invasive species to flourish. This, in turn, affects the feeding, reproduction, and migration patterns of wildlife species higher in the food chain.

Manatees congregate in the warm water discharged by an electric power plant in Florida. Power plants are a major source of thermal pollution, which can disrupt the balance of surrounding ecosystems.

Finally, the industrial emissions and urban runoff that are the main sources of thermal pollution may also introduce toxic chemicals into water bodies that make them unsafe for human use.

Since half of all the water withdrawn in the United States is used to cool electrical power plants, using less electricity is a good way to reduce thermal pollution. Industrial facilities can also limit their thermal pollution by storing the heated discharge water in cooling towers or collecting ponds before releasing it into the environment. Finally, zoning and development policies that preserve shoreline vegetation and prevent urban runoff can also protect aquatic ecosystems from thermal pollution.

Radioactivity and Health

Radiation is a form of energy that is emitted in particles or rays. People are exposed to radiation from numerous sources, including sunlight, atomic bomb blasts, nuclear weapons tests, nuclear power plant accidents, mining operations, radon gas from rocks and soil, food that is irradiated to kill harmful bacteria, medical X-rays, and electromagnetic fields from power lines, microwave ovens, television sets, and computer screens. The energy that comes from radioactive materials is absorbed by living cells, and this energy sometimes changes the cells' structure in ways that cause them to mutate and become cancerous. The health effects of radiation depend on the individual, so scientists cannot be entirely certain about what doses of radiation exposure are safe.

There is no doubt, however, that exposure to high levels of radiation poses a severe health threat. When the U.S. military dropped an atomic bomb on the Japanese city of Hiroshima during World War II, for instance, eighty thousand people were killed instantly, but tens of thousands more died over the next few weeks from exposure to radiation. In the short term, survivors experienced burns, hair loss, anemia, bleeding, and diarrhea. Over the long term, they experienced high rates of birth defects, leukemia, and cancers of the thyroid, breast, lungs, and salivary glands.

Civilian uses of nuclear energy have caused deadly health effects as well. The world's worst nuclear power disaster occurred in 1986 at Chernobyl in the Soviet Union, when a reactor exploded and sent radioactive materials high into the air. The fallout spread more than 1,250 miles (2,000km) and affected citizens of twenty countries. The plant workers, firefighters, and cleanup crews that responded to the disaster were exposed to high levels of radiation. Thirty-one people died immediately, and thousands of others suffered long-term health problems.

Mining for the uranium needed to produce nuclear power and nuclear weapons also generates dangerous radioactive waste materials. About 97 percent of all radioactive waste takes the form of tailings, or crushed rock that is left over after the valuable mineral has been extracted. These tailings often accumulate in large piles near mining operations, many of which can be found in the western United States. Several storage sites are located along the Colorado River, which supplies drinking water to Los Angeles and other major cities. Millions of tons of radioactive tailings have blown or washed into the river over the years. At one time the tailings were even used in the construction of roads, parking lots, homes, and schools.

Radioactive waste has taken a toll on the health of the Navajo Nation, where major uranium mining occurred during the 1950s and 1960s. Many Navajo men worked in the mines, while Navajo children played atop the huge piles of

An aerial photo from 1986 shows the damage at the Chernobyl Nuclear Power Plant in Ukraine after the worst nuclear power accident in history.

tailings and the community's livestock grazed nearby. After inhaling radioactive dust and drinking contaminated water for years, the Navajo people have experienced high rates of lung cancer—even though the disease was virtually unknown among them before they were exposed to radiation. Some Navajo families have received assistance from the U.S. government under the Radiation Exposure Compensation Act, which was enacted in 1990.

The health risks associated with radioactive waste make it very difficult to store these materials safely. It takes twenty-four thousand years for uranium to break down naturally in the environment, and the mineral continues to emit radioactivity throughout that time. The U.S. government attempted to solve this problem by creating a centralized national storage site beneath Yucca Mountain in Nevada. The area's dry climate, stable geology, and distance from major population centers made it seem like an attractive alternative. But the plan ran into intense opposition from local residents and environmental groups, who warned about the dangers of transporting radioactive waste across the country. Federal funding for development of the Yucca Mountain site ended in 2011, so most radioactive waste continues to be stored onsite at nuclear power stations or in state-run facilities.

Solid Waste and Health

In addition to the controversies surrounding disposal of hazardous and radioactive wastes, people also face problems getting rid of the massive amounts of ordinary solid waste that they generate. Around 65 percent of the trash created in the United States, or 164 million tons (149 million t), ends up being dumped in landfills or burned in incinerators each year. Both of these disposal methods result in emissions of "greenhouse gases," such as methane and carbon dioxide, that trap heat in the earth's atmosphere and contribute to global climate change. Improper disposal

Recycling is an important component of responsible solid waste management, and many municipalities provide a variety of solid waste disposal options.

of solid waste, meanwhile, can pollute air and water and release toxic chemicals into the environment.

To minimize the impact of garbage disposal on the environment and human health, EPA experts recommend that communities use an integrated solid waste management approach. This type of program involves several different activities, including waste prevention, recycling, composting, controlled burning, and landfilling. The first step, waste prevention, aims to reduce the amount of garbage that people produce. It involves buying durable goods that last a long time, looking for products that have minimal packaging, and switching from disposable to reusable products. Waste prevention helps protect the environment by reducing consumption of natural resources as well as eliminating sources of garbage.

In addition to reducing purchases and reusing products, recycling is an important step in solid waste management. Recycling prevents materials like metal, glass, and plastic from being disposed of as trash. Instead, these raw materials are removed from the waste stream and converted into useful items. By keeping garbage out of landfills, recycling helps reduce greenhouse gas emissions. Some products that contain hazardous chemicals—such as computers, batteries, tires, and used motor oil—can also be recycled to prevent toxins from entering water supplies. Many state and local governments support recycling efforts by organizing curbside pickup, recycling centers, or hazardous waste drop-off sites.

Composting is a method of recycling organic matter, such as food scraps, leaves, and grass clippings. These materials are mixed with water and allowed to decompose with the help of natural bacteria, fungi, and worms. Composting creates a nutrient-rich substance called humus that can improve the quality of soil and reduce the need for chemical fertilizers and pesticides. It is a valuable substance used in vegetable gardens, landscaping, and erosion control. Composting also prevents organic materials from reaching landfills, which helps reduce greenhouse gas emissions.

When solid waste cannot be recycled or composted, it may be burned in a high-temperature incinerator. Although combustion generates air pollution, this can be reduced through the use of scrubbers and filters. Combustion also helps reduce the amount of solid waste that ends up in landfills. In some cases, garbage is burned in place of coal or other fossil fuels to generate electricity.

The final option in an integrated solid waste management approach is disposing of garbage in a landfill. As opposed to uncontrolled dumping of trash—which can contaminate water and soil and attract unwanted rodents

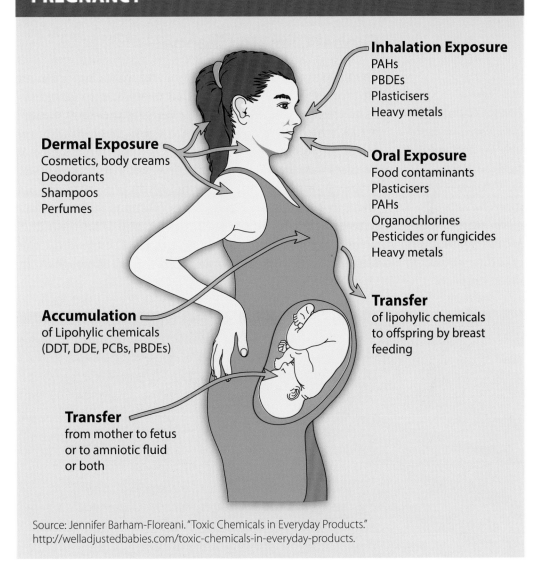

SOURCES OF EXPOSURE TO TOXIC CHEMICALS DURING PREGNANCY

Inhalation Exposure
PAHs
PBDEs
Plasticisers
Heavy metals

Dermal Exposure
Cosmetics, body creams
Deodorants
Shampoos
Perfumes

Oral Exposure
Food contaminants
Plasticisers
PAHs
Organochlorines
Pesticides or fungicides
Heavy metals

Transfer
of lipohylic chemicals
to offspring by breast
feeding

Accumulation
of Lipohylic chemicals
(DDT, DDE, PCBs, PBDEs)

Transfer
from mother to fetus
or to amniotic fluid
or both

Source: Jennifer Barham-Floreani. "Toxic Chemicals in Everyday Products."
http://welladjustedbabies.com/toxic-chemicals-in-everyday-products.

and insects—well-designed landfills are relatively safe and environmentally responsible. Landfills are lined to prevent liquids from seeping out into the soil or groundwater. They are also vented to allow methane gas—which is produced during the decomposition of organic materials—to escape.

Although it is considered a greenhouse gas that contributes to global climate change, methane is also highly flammable. Some landfill operators recover the methane gas and burn it to generate electricity.

Global Climate Change

Solid waste disposal, air pollution, and toxic chemicals can all produce greenhouse gases that contribute to global climate change. One of the worst offenders is carbon dioxide (CO_2), which is produced through decomposition or burning of organic matter. Although CO_2 is often mentioned as an alarming form of pollution, it is not harmful in itself. Trace amounts of the gas are naturally present in the air, and it is essential to life on earth. Humans and other animals exhale CO_2 when they breathe, and trees and other plants take it in and convert it to oxygen. Carbon dioxide also plays an important role in the upper atmosphere by

Forests in Indonesia are cleared to make way for agricultural fields in 2014. Such deforestation contributes to global warming by increasing the levels of carbon dioxide in the atmosphere.

helping to trap heat from the sun in order to maintain the planet's average temperature.

The problem is that carbon dioxide levels in the atmosphere have been increasing for decades, creating a "greenhouse effect" that has contributed to a steady increase in average temperatures around the world. Most scientists believe that human activities are responsible for this global climate change—primarily the combustion of fossil fuels like petroleum and coal, which produces CO_2, and the destruction of forests, which allows more CO_2 to enter the atmosphere. The levels of CO_2 have more than doubled in the past two hundred years, since the technological developments of the Industrial Revolution.

The increase in worldwide average temperatures has contributed to melting polar ice caps, receding glaciers, disappearing permafrost, rising sea levels, and more extreme weather, including severe storms and droughts. Many of these changes have the potential to threaten human safety and health. As average temperatures rise, for example, tropical diseases such as malaria and dengue fever can spread to new regions of the world. Hurricanes, tornadoes, and other deadly storm systems can destroy homes and take human lives. Droughts and heat waves can cause famine by destroying crops and killing livestock. Flooding from rising sea levels can cause sewer systems to overflow and allow bacteria and debris to enter drinking water supplies. Finally, higher global temperatures can lead to poor air quality by increasing the production of allergy-causing pollen and ground-level ozone.

The United Nations (UN) has led the worldwide response to the threat of climate change. In 1997 the UN's Intergovernmental Panel on Climate Change produced the Kyoto Protocol, a treaty that established national targets for reducing greenhouse gas emissions. The European Union and many individual countries launched their own programs for eliminating harmful pollution and finding alternative forms of energy. But some countries—including the United States and China, which together account for 45 percent of the world's greenhouse gas emissions—refused to sign the treaty and resisted making the difficult and expensive changes it required. Some people claimed that global climate change was not related to human activities, while others argued that implementing the measures would cause economic hardship.

In 2014, however, the United States and China announced a historic agreement to reduce their carbon dioxide emissions. "It's the agreement that people have been waiting for, for a long time," said Jake Schmidt of the Natural Resources Defense Council. "It's the two biggest emitters, the two largest economies, the two biggest drags on agreement over the years. For them to step up and say we're going to take deep actions, it will send a powerful signal to countries around the world."[20]

CHAPTER 5

Preventing Pollution and Protecting Health

It often seems as though the news is full of stories about smog choking cities, sewage overflowing into rivers, toxic chemicals found in household products, and the dangerous effects of global climate change. When confronted with all the harmful effects of environmental pollution, it is easy to feel overwhelmed. Yet there are many positive trends that give people reason to be optimistic about the future. There are also many steps ordinary citizens can take to help prevent pollution and protect their health.

Whereas most studies about the health effects of pollution once focused on adults, more scientists are now researching the harmful effects on children's development. Lawmakers are beginning to pay attention to the results of these studies and introduce bills to prohibit the use of toxic chemicals in toys, clothing, and other items used by children. Rather than waiting for regulations, some forward-thinking businesses are taking the initiative to eliminate hazardous substances in the products they sell. Other companies are working with suppliers to develop environmentally friendly production processes and reduce packaging. More consumers are demanding pesticide-free organic foods and chemical-free household goods.

Some people resist making changes because they do

Choosing organic foods, which minimize contact with pesticides and other chemicals, is one way for consumers to protect their health.

not believe that individual actions make a difference. But minimizing exposure to environmental pollutants can provide health benefits—especially for children. Plus, if enough individuals demand cleaner air and water and environmentally safe products, then polluting industries may be forced to change their ways. "People often blame science, industry, and government for pollution. But what about the public itself? All opinion polls show that we want to be rid of hazardous waste. Yet we do not want plants near us that treat such waste. Nor do we wish to give up all the chemicals that make our lives easier, even though their production creates hazardous compounds," Stephen J. Zipko wrote in *Toxic Threat*. "Citizens in a democracy must accept the responsibility of establishing safe standards for hazardous substances. Only society can decide if certain levels of disease are acceptably small, or if the cost of a control measure is worth the burden it will impose on taxpayers."[21]

Minimizing Exposure to Pollution

Although it is impossible to avoid exposure to pollution entirely, there are many ways to minimize the health risks.

Environmental Impacts of Bottled Water

Although bottled water may be convenient, it is a bad choice for the environment. It takes about 4 ounces (125ml) of crude oil to make one 16-ounce (500ml) plastic water bottle—or the equivalent of filling that bottle one-quarter full of oil. Since more than 200 billion bottles of water are sold worldwide each year, this amounts to more than 50 billion barrels of oil devoted to bottle manufacturing—enough to fuel 3 million cars for a year. In the United States, which is the world's largest consumer of bottled water, 1,500 bottles are sold every second.

Bottling water uses other resources as well. For instance, 2 gallons (7.5L) of water are wasted for every 1 gallon (3.75L) that is filtered and bottled. Bottling plants often draw down groundwater supplies and create shortages for local residents. Some people drink bottled water because they believe it is healthier, but tap water is actually held to stricter quality standards in the United States. In addition, plastic water bottles contain chemicals—including bisphenol A and phthalates—that have been found to be hazardous to human health.

Another problem with using bottled water is that it generates huge amounts of trash. Although recycling helps, only one out of every six plastic water bottles ends up being recycled. The rest end up in landfills, where the plastic takes hundreds of years to disintegrate, or as trash along roadsides or in parks, rivers, and oceans. To make a better choice for the environment, experts recommend carrying tap water in a reusable, BPA-free plastic or stainless steel bottle.

Plastic water bottles often end up as litter in parks, along roadsides, or in rivers or oceans.

In the case of air pollution, one good strategy is to pay attention to weather forecasts and remain indoors on ozone action days or when levels of pollen or particulate matter are high. When outdoors, it is helpful to avoid busy streets with lots of motor vehicle traffic, as well as school bus lanes full of idling buses. To reduce the risk of inhaling exhaust fumes at home, never leave a car running in the garage.

Of course, not all air pollution comes from outdoor sources—indoor air pollution can also pose a threat to human health. One of the best methods of clearing out pollutants from homes or offices is to open the windows regularly and allow fresh air to circulate. It is also helpful to remove shoes when entering the house to avoid tracking in bacteria and toxins, to vacuum carpets and furniture frequently, and to change the filters on air conditioners and furnaces on a regular schedule. Finally, experts recommend against using cleansers and disinfectants that contain toxic chemicals, as well as products that contain strong fragrances, such as air fresheners. Instead, they suggest using natural cleansers such as vinegar and baking soda.

One of the first steps in minimizing exposure to water pollution is to find out what chemicals are present in local drinking water supplies. Public water utilities are required to publish regular reports on water quality that list the levels of certain contaminants. People who draw water from a private well should have it tested regularly and install filters as needed to remove harmful chemicals. Experts also recommend checking the websites of state environmental authorities to get information about bacteria levels before swimming in lakes or allowing children to play on beaches.

Toxic chemicals can be found in a wide variety of products, so it can be difficult to avoid exposure to them. To eliminate some potential sources of toxins, experts recommend choosing clothing, carpets, and furniture made from natural fabrics, without any flame retardant chemicals or stain resistant coatings. They also suggest that consumers avoid using nonstick cookware treated with Teflon or other perfluorinated chemicals, which release toxic fumes and particles when they get too hot. Safer cookware choices include cast iron, stainless steel, glass, or ceramic.

Many household cleaning products contain hazardous chemicals. To avoid inhaling or absorbing toxins, it is best to dilute them with water, wear gloves, and use them in a well-ventilated room without children present. Another option is to try homemade, environmentally friendly alternatives made from vinegar, baking soda, lemon juice, or

Replacing cleaning products with natural alternatives, such as lemon juice and baking soda, is one way to reduce exposure to hazardous household chemicals.

other natural materials. Flea collars, dips, and sprays for pets contain high doses of pesticides. Experts recommend getting rid of fleas and ticks by bathing, brushing, and vacuuming pets instead. Finally, potentially dangerous chemicals can be found in many brands of cosmetics, nail polish, perfume, lotions, and even sunscreen. Consumers should read labels carefully, choose products with a minimum of unrecognizable ingredients, and avoid products with artificial fragrances or dyes.

Food products and packaging are another major source of harmful chemicals. To limit exposure to pesticides, experts recommend buying organic produce or scrubbing nonorganic produce with a vegetable brush before eating. Many species of fish contain mercury or persistent organic pollutants like PCBs. It is important to choose types of fish that are low in contaminants and follow the consumption guidelines for specific bodies of water. Finally, food packaging and storage containers can contain endocrine-disrupting chemicals like bisphenol A (BPA) and phthalates that can leach into foods and beverages. Experts recommend choosing glass containers instead of plastic whenever possible—especially for babies—and never microwaving foods in plastic. The Environmental Working Group (www.ewg.org) offers guidelines for choosing food, personal care, and household products with a minimum of harmful chemicals.

Minimizing Impact on the Environment

There are many steps people can take to reduce their own personal environmental impact, which in turn helps eliminate sources of pollution. Perhaps the most important step is to conserve energy whenever possible. Coal-fired electrical power plants are among the worst sources of air pollution, so every kilowatt of energy conserved helps reduce emissions. Some possible methods for conserving energy include turning off lights, computers, and other electrical equipment when not in use; installing energy-efficient lightbulbs and appliances; and adjusting the thermostat by a few degrees. Consumers can also support efforts to develop renewable energy sources that are not dependent on fossil fuels, such as wind, solar, and water power. Automobiles are another significant source of air pollution and carbon dioxide emissions. Some tips to reduce their environmental impact include switching to environmentally friendly means of transportation, such as walking or riding a bicycle; carpooling, ride-sharing, or taking public transportation; buying electric, hybrid, or energy-efficient vehicles; maintaining vehicles and keeping tires fully inflated; and combining multiple errands into a single trip.

To help keep water supplies clean and abundant, people should never flush prescription medicines down the toilet or dump oil, gasoline, paints, solvents, or other hazardous materials in drains or sewers. These items—as well as computer equipment, televisions, air conditioners, refrigerators,

Commuting by bicycle or on public transit systems instead of by car can reduce one's environmental impact.

Students Against Plastic Grocery Sacks

When members of the environmental club at an Idaho high school picked up trash in their community, they found that the biggest source of litter was plastic grocery bags. "We do all these trash cleanups and saw them littered all over the city, in the trees, in the road, in my front yard," said sixteen-year-old junior Maggie Williams. "It's kind of disgusting."

People in the United States use an estimated 100 billion of the lightweight plastic sacks per year—a significant portion of the approximately 500 billion used worldwide. The bags are convenient and recyclable, and they can be reused for everything from carrying dirty gym clothes to picking up dog poop. But millions of the bags end up littering the environment, where they create an eyesore, suffocate or strangle wildlife, and leach toxic chemicals.

The Idaho students responded to the problem by introducing a ballot initiative that asked voters to prohibit area retailers from providing plastic bags to their customers. Although voters ultimately rejected an outright ban, the publicity surrounding the issue encouraged many local residents to switch to reusable bags. More than 140 communities across the United States—including Los Angeles, San Francisco, and Washington, D.C.—have implemented measures to discourage plastic-bag usage that have resulted in reductions of 60 to 90 percent.

Roya Camp. "Students in Hailey, Idaho, Look to Sack Plastic Grocery Bags." *Idaho Business Review*, September 30, 2011.

cell phones, batteries, and other products that may contain mercury, lead, and other harmful chemicals—should be disposed of properly at a recycling center. To reduce the risk of harmful chemicals entering lakes and rivers from yard and driveway runoff, experts recommend avoiding the use of artificial fertilizers, pesticides, and weed killers; picking up pet waste; and maintaining cars to prevent them from leaking fluids. Tips for conserving water include taking showers instead of baths, turning off the tap while washing dishes or brushing teeth, going to a commercial car wash instead of using a hose, and watering lawns in the morning or evening to reduce evaporation.

Many other simple, everyday choices people make can also have an impact on the environment. People can make a difference in their communities by cleaning up trash, recycling, planting trees and native plants, buying secondhand or environmentally friendly products whenever possible, and supporting local, organic farms. Finally, individuals can increase their influence by becoming politically active. Some options include joining an established environmental group, starting a club at a school or in the community, and writing letters or sending emails to lawmakers or corporations encouraging them to be environmentally responsible.

Some experts believe that the key to protecting the environment will be a grassroots movement focused on children's health. "A social movement whose mission is community and the health of American children can pursue changes in consumer action, present a unified body to confront corporations singly or by industry, locally or nationally, use the unbounded capacities of the Internet to get out news and information overlooked by the corporate media, provide practical advice to parents, learn from one another's lawsuits," Philip and Alice Shabecoff wrote in *Poisoned Profits*. "This social movement can turn into a new, irresistible political force."[22]

NOTES

Introduction: The Connection Between Pollution and Health

1. Quoted in John Vidal. "WHO: Air Pollution 'Is Single Biggest Environmental Health Risk.'" *The Guardian*, March 25, 2014. www.theguardian.com/environment/2014/mar/25/air-pollution-single-biggest-environmental-health-risk-who.

2. McKay Jenkins. *What's Gotten into Us? Staying Healthy in a Toxic World*. New York: Random House, 2011, p. 13.

3. Sandra Steingraber. *Raising Elijah: Protecting Our Children in an Age of Environmental Crisis*. Boston, MA: Da Capo, 2011, p. xv.

4. United Nations Environment Programme, Collaborating Center on Energy and Environment (UC-CEE). "Environmental Protection." UCCEE.org, n.d. www.uccee.org/Environmental_Protection.html.

Chapter 1: Air Pollution and Health

5. Quoted in Paul Brown. "Fifty Years after the Great Smog, a New Killer Arises." *The Guardian*, November 30, 2002. www.theguardian.com/uk_news/story/0,3604,850909,00.html.

6. Quoted in Ann Murray. "Smog Deaths in 1948 Led to Clean Air Laws." NPR, April 22, 2009. www.npr.org/templates/story/story.php?storyId=103359330.

Chapter 2: Water Pollution and Health

7. Quoted in John Noble Wilford. "How Epidemics Helped Shape the Modern Metropolis." *New York Times*, April 15, 2008. www.nytimes.com/2008/04/15/science/15chol.html?_r=0.

8. Quoted in Jack Doyle. "'Burn On, Big River…': Cuyahoga River Fires." PopHistoryDig.com, May 12, 2014 www.pophistorydig.com/topics/burn-on-big-river-cuyahoga-river-fires/.

9. Quoted in Dashka Slater. "This Much Mercury…" *Sierra*, November–December 2011. http://vault.sierraclub.org/sierra/201111/mercury.aspx

10. Quoted in Daniel Lak. "Exxon Valdez Spill Effects Linger Twenty-

Five Years On." *Al Jazeera*, March 24, 2014. www.aljazeera.com/indepth/features/2014/03/exxon-valdez-spill-25-years-alaska-2014324101725585439.html.

11. Quoted in "Twenty-Five Years of the Safe Drinking Water Act: History and Trends." U.S. Environmental Protection Agency, December 1999. http://permanent.access.gpo.gov/websites/epagov/www.epa.gov/safewater/sdwa/trends.html.

12. Quoted in Charles Duhigg. "Clean Water Laws Are Neglected, at a Cost in Suffering." *New York Times*, September 12, 2009. www.nytimes.com/2009/09/13/us/13water.html?pagewanted=all&_r=0.

Chapter 3: Hazardous Chemicals and Health

13. Rachel Carson. *Silent Spring*. Boston: Houghton Mifflin, 1962, p. 13.

14. Quoted in Eckardt C. Beck. "The Love Canal Tragedy." *EPA Journal*, January 1979. www2.epa.gov/aboutepa/love-canal-tragedy.

15. Quoted in Sam Howe Verhovek. "After Ten Years, the Trauma of Love Canal Continues." *New York Times*, August 5, 1988. www.nytimes.com/1988/08/05/nyregion/after-10-years-the-trauma-of-love-canal-continues.html.

16. Herbert L. Needleman. *Raising Children Toxic Free*. New York: Farrar, Straus, and Giroux, 1994.

17. Quoted in Bill Moyers. "Sandra Steingraber's War on Toxic Trespassers." *Moyers and Company*, April 19, 2013. http://billmoyers.com/segment/sandra-steingrabers-war-on-toxic-trespassers/.

Chapter 4: Other Types of Pollution and Health

18. Quoted in Jonathan Orlando. "Vehicle Noise and the Toll on People." *Culture Change*, n.d. www.culturechange.org/issue19/vehicle_noise.htm.

19. Quoted in Holly Haworth. "And Incredibly Bright." *Earth Island Journal*, Spring 2013. www.earthisland.org/journal/index.php/eij/article/and_incredibly_bright/.

20. Quoted in Rebecca Leber. "The World Has Waited for the U.S. and China to Take Action on Global Climate Change. They Just Did." *New Republic*, November 12, 2014. www.newrepublic.com/article/120242/us-and-china-reach-agreement-climate-change.

Chapter 5: Preventing Pollution and Protecting Health

21. Stephen J. Zipko. *Toxic Threat: How Hazardous Substances Poison Our Lives*. Englewood Cliffs, NJ: Julian Messner, 1990, pp. 219–220.

22. Philip Shabecoff and Alice Shabecoff. *Poisoned Profits: The Toxic Assault on Our Children*. New York: Random House, 2008, p. 257.

biodegradable: Able to be broken down or decomposed by bacteria and other living organisms.

carcinogen: A substance that is capable of causing cancer.

combustion: The process of burning fuel or matter.

contaminant: A substance that has a negative impact on living organisms when it is present in the environment.

effluent: Liquid waste that is discharged into a body of water.

emission: The discharge or release of a substance into the environment.

eutrophication: A process in which a body of water receives excess nutrients, which stimulates the growth of algae and reduces the oxygen available for aquatic plants and animals.

fossil fuel: A fuel that is formed from the decay of dead plants and animals in the earth, such as coal, oil, and natural gas.

greenhouse gas: A gas that helps trap heat in the earth's atmosphere and contributes to global climate change.

hydrocarbon: A compound made up of hydrogen and carbon that is found in many fossil fuels.

industrialization: The introduction of manufacturing and technology into a country or region.

leach: To be released from a substance such as soil when liquid passes through; refers to chemicals.

nonpoint source pollution: A situation in which the contaminants entering air or water come from multiple small sources spread over a wide area.

pathogen: A biological agent that causes illness or disease.

point source pollution: A situation in which the contaminants entering air or water come from a single, easily-identifiable source.

pollutant: A potentially harmful substance that is introduced into the environment.

pollution: The introduction of substances into the environment that would not normally be present and that are potentially harmful.

regulate: To make rules or laws to control something.

runoff: Rainfall or snowmelt that is not absorbed by soil and flows over the ground to enter water bodies.

solid waste: Garbage or trash that is discarded by households and businesses.

toxic: Extremely harmful or poisonous to humans or animals.

Agency for Toxic Substances and Disease Registry (ATSDR)

U.S. Centers for Disease Control and Prevention
4770 Buford Hwy NE
Atlanta, GA 30341
phone: (800) 232-4636
website: www.atsdr.cdc.gov

ATSDR is the U.S. government agency that helps protect people from the health effects of exposure to toxic chemicals. It conducts public health assessments of toxic waste sites, responds to releases of hazardous substances, provides education and training concerning hazardous substances, and maintains a registry of information about toxic chemicals.

Center for Health, Environment, and Justice (CHEJ)

PO Box 6806
Falls Church, VA 22040
phone: (703) 237-2249
website: www.chej.org

CHEJ provides training and organizational assistance to help people take action to prevent exposure to environmental pollution and build healthier communities. "By organizing one school, one neighborhood, one community at a time, CHEJ is making the world cleaner and healthier for all of us," according to its website.

Environmental Working Group (EWG)

1436 U Street NW, Suite 100
Washington, DC 20009
phone: (202) 667-6982
website: www.ewg.org

EWG conducts investigations and research on toxic chemicals and environmental health, food and agriculture, and water and energy. It offers guides and ratings to help consumers choose the healthiest and most environmentally-friendly foods, cosmetics, household cleaners, and other products.

Physicians for Social Responsibility (PSR)

1111 14th Street NW, Suite 700
Washington, DC 20005
phone: (202) 667-4260
website: www.psr.org

PSR uses medical and public health expertise to address the dangers that threaten communities, including air and water pollution, toxic chemicals, and global climate change. Its goal is to "create a healthy, just, and peaceful world for both the present and future generations."

Union of Concerned Scientists (UCS)

2 Brattle Square
Cambridge, MA 02138-3780
phone: (617) 547-5552
website: www.ucsusa.org

The motto of UCS is "science for a healthy planet and safer world." Its scientists and engineers work to develop alternative methods of power generation, agricultural production, transportation, and manufacturing that protect the environment and human health.

U.S. Environmental Protection Agency (EPA)

1200 Pennsylvania Ave. NW
Washington, DC 20460
phone: (202) 272-0167
website: www.epa.gov

The EPA is the main U.S. government regulatory body concerned with environmental pollution. It maintains statistics about pollution, provides information about the latest scientific research and technological developments, and offers activities for students and teachers.

Books and Articles

Zachary Chastain. *Industrial Chemicals and Health*. New York: Alpha-House, 2009. Intended for students, this book provides a readable overview of the ways in which environmental toxins affect people.

Bridget Heos. *Polluted Water and Your Vital Organs*. New York: Rosen, 2013. This helpful book examines the many impacts of water pollution on human health and the larger environment.

Nancy Irwin Maxwell. *Understanding Environmental Health: How We Live in the World*. Burlington, MA: Jones and Bartlett Learning, 2014. This innovative textbook explores how the modern lifestyle and consumer choices create environmental and public health hazards.

Emily Sanna. *Air Pollution and Health*. New York: AlphaHouse, 2009. This book offers students a clear and comprehensive guide to the sources and types of air pollution, along with facts about the health effects of inhaling airborne contaminants.

Rae Simons. *A Kid's Guide to Pollution and How It Can Make You Sick*. Vestal, NY: Village Earth Press, 2013. Intended for students, this book examines the connection between health and exposure to pollutants, with a special emphasis on young, developing bodies.

Websites

Abandoned Environment (www.uccee .org). This website, maintained by the United Nations Environment Programme's Collaborating Centre on Energy and Environment, offers a series of informative articles about environmental pollution, its effects, and strategies for a sustainable future.

Climate Hot Map: Global Warming Effects around the World (www .climatehotmap.org/global-warming -effects/health.html). Operated by the Union of Concerned Scientists, this website explores the effects of global climate change on human health and the environment. It also includes detailed maps and suggested actions to address the threat posed by increasing average temperatures.

Environmental Pollution (www.who .int/topics/environmental_pollution /en/). The World Health Organization provides fact sheets about various pollution issues as well as links to detailed reports, activities, and news and information.

Healthy Child Healthy World (http://healthychild.org). This nonprofit organization aims to give parents information and resources to help them make lifestyle choices that will reduce their children's toxic chemical exposure at home and in the community.

Protecting Children's Environmental Health (www2.epa.gov/children). Maintained by the U.S. Environmental Protection Agency, this website offers facts and information for parents and healthcare providers, access to the latest scientific research and government regulations, and links to resources for improving environmental quality at home and at school.

Scorecard: The Pollution Information Site (http://scorecard.good guide.com). This useful website provides detailed maps and information about toxic chemical releases, Superfund sites, hazardous air pollutants, and other environmental threats across the United States. Users can also enter their own ZIP code to view a pollution report for their county.

INDEX

M

Martin County (KY), 46–47, *47*
Massey Energy, 46–47
Mercury, 43
Methane gas, 79–80
Mining, *62*, 64, 75–76
Mississippi River, 46
Montreal Protocol, 29
Motor vehicles. *See* Transportation

N

National ambient air quality standards,
    15, 26
Navajo Nation, 75–76
New Delhi (India), 16, *25*
New York (NY), 33
Nitrogen oxides, 18–19
Noise pollution, 66–69, *67*
Nonpoint source pollution, 16–17, 35–37
Nuclear energy, 74–75, *75*
Nutrient pollutants, 39, 46

O

Ocean dumping, 37
Oil spills, *39*, 40, 45
Organic foods, *84,* 88
Organic material pollutants, 40
Ozone (pollutant), 19, 30
Ozone layer, 29, *29*

P

Packaging, 88
Particulate matter, 19, 21, 30
Pathogens, 40, 43–45
PCBs, 57
Persistent organic pollutants, 55–57
Pesticides, 39–40, 42–43, 54, 55–56
Pharmaceutical drugs, 51
Plastics, 58, *61*, 85, *85*, 90
Point source pollution, 16, 35–36, 46

Port Neches (TX), air pollution in, 23
Power plants
    energy conservation, 88–89
    pollution, 28, *28*, 73, *73*, 74–75, *75*
Pregnancy, *79*
Prevention, pollution
    environmental impacts, minimizing,
        88–91
    health impacts, minimizing, 86–88
    solid wastes, 77–78, 85
    See also Laws and regulations
Public awareness, 14–15, 34, 51–53, 90, 91

R

Radiation Exposure Compensation Act,
    76
Radioactivity, 74–76
Radon, 22
Recycling, *77,* 78
Registration, Evaluation, Authorisation
    and Restriction of Chemicals
    (REACH), 64
Regulations. *See* Laws and regulations
Research, 59–60
Risk factors for air pollution health issues,
    24
Runoff, 35–36, *36*, 38, 42–43, 46

S

Safe Drinking Water Act, 47–48
Secondhand smoke, 21, *22*
Sewage treatment systems, 35
Sick building syndrome, 24
Skin cancer, 29
Smog, *11*, 14–16, *15*, *25*
Smoking, 21, *22*
Solid waste, 37, 76–80, 90
Sources of pollution, 16–18, 35–38, 53–55
Stockholm Convention, 55
Sulfur dioxide, 18
Superfund Act, 53, 64

PICTURE CREDITS

Laurie Collier Hillstrom is the author of more than twenty books in the areas of biography, history, and current issues. Recent works include *Hot Topics: Natural Disasters* (Lucent Books, 2014) and *Defining Moments: Jackie Robinson and the Integration of Baseball* (Omnigraphics, 2013). She lives in Brighton, Michigan, with her husband and twin daughters.